## What people are saying about Joshua Mills and *Moving in Glory Realms...*

"Joshua Mills is in passionate pursuit of the God of glory. One cannot passionately pursue God without experiencing a metamorphosis from the inside out, a change that touches the whole of your being, spirit, soul, and body. We are living in days of fresh release and renewal, and Joshua is out there on the living edge as a herald of the 'more' that God is calling us both from and to. Let Joshua take you on a journey into what he has uniquely called the 'glory realms,' and allow yourself to begin moving in this amazing, glorious life of this age of the Spirit!"

—*Bishop Mark J. Chironna, MA, DMin*
Church On The Living Edge
Mark Chironna Ministries
Longwood, Florida

"*Moving in Glory Realms* is a must read! I can't think of anyone more qualified to write it than Joshua Mills. He, his wife, and family don't just talk it—they live it! I am confident that when you read this book you will receive an invitation to higher levels of encounter, Spirit-empowered revelation, and anointed impartation. *Moving in Glory Realms* is for every believer to experience—it is for you!"

—*Dr. Patricia King*
Founder, Patricia King Ministries
Maricopa, Arizona

"This is a foundational book to 'prep' for the glory, not the tribulation!"

—*Sid Roth*
Host, *It's Supernatural!*

W9-AKV-742

"In my years of ministry around the globe, I have found that everything is transformed in the wonderful presence of the Holy Spirit we call *the glory*. It is in the realm of God's presence that we are transformed, circumstances bow, and one word can make the impossible possible. I believe we are now, more than ever before, stepping into the prophetic promise given in Isaiah 6:3: *'The whole earth is full of His glory.'* *Moving in Glory Realms* comes at a very strategic time for God's church. A fresh wave of glory for the end-time harvest is here, and God is raising up His glory-carriers to minister God's healing, salvation, and deliverance. *Moving in Glory Realms* will serve as a catalyst to awaken hunger for God's presence, and it will lay out a biblical foundation for you to live and move in greater levels of faith, anointing, and glory. May the Lord open up this realm to you as you study the pages of this book."

—*Mahesh Chavda*
Senior Pastor, All Nations Church
Charlotte, North Carolina

"Those who have met Joshua Mills instantly discover his passion for the glory of God. His new book, *Moving in Glory Realms*, is saturated with stories of extraordinary experiences and magnificent insight into those realms of God's glory. Though there have been several books written on this subject, few if any match the depth of Joshua's vision and comprehension of divine presence. It will challenge you and compel you to seek His glory."

—*Rev. Bobby Schuller*
Lead Pastor, Shepherd's Grove, Orange County, California
Host, *The Hour of Power with Bobby Schuller*

"My friend Joshua Mills has a way of making the supernatural natural, but certainly never ordinary. His boyish grin, dancing eyes, otherworldly music, and humble heart disarms the most hardened, callused souls among us. His passion for God is so salted with desire that he makes us thirsty for fresh water and real presence. Joshua answers our tough spiritual questions with textbook precision and scriptural accuracy, while sprinkling his responses with a dollop of childlike wonder, awe, and delicious mystery. Do you have a pocketful of questions concerning the glory realms? What about the ministry of angels? Are signs and wonders for today? How do we open up the ancient windows of financial provision? I encourage you to have a pen and paper handy as you study and enjoy the wisdom from this seasoned prophetic voice."

—*Reba Rambo-McGuire*
Singer/songwriter and Grammy Award-winning recording artist
Franklin, Tennessee

"*Moving in Glory Realms* perfectly sums up Joshua Mills's life and ministry because it is the point at which all his experience and understanding of God meet together and kiss. This book contains a wealth of small nuggets of revelatory truth, as well as a panoramic overview of the glorious, redemptive work of God, as revealed in the Scriptures and in the experience of the body of Christ. Joshua is a forerunner of the work of the Holy Spirit in these end times, and he has chosen to reveal much of what he has learned in this book. Read it, digest it, do it, and then start the process all over again. Glory!"

—*Joan Hunter*
Author, Healing Evangelist

"Joshua Mills walks in realms of glory that always astonish me! I experienced some realms of glory in 1981, but after I met Joshua in 2009, there was an immediate acceleration of access and administration of glory in and through my life. The realms in which he lives are contagious, and he imparts this glory with such a spirit of rest, humility, and fun. His friendship and ministry have impacted our church in Hong Kong in so many wonderful ways and have activated open doors for Glenda and me into nations. Joshua is a frontrunner, and I can assure you that as you read this book, you will transition out of any inferior jurisdictions and into the superior jurisdictions of supernatural glory."

—*Rob Rufus*
Senior Pastor, City Church International
Hong Kong

"I'm always looking for books that capture how we should think, believe, and act in this new era we have entered. Joshua Mills brilliantly sets forth understanding, recognizing, and moving in glory realms through his explanations, revelation, and experiences. This book has an amazing touch of life on it, and I felt myself lifted up into the realms he was explaining, as well as challenged to reach into greater realms. I so value Joshua, a man of great integrity and love. He has such a great heart to enlarge the spiritual eyes and understanding of this generation."

—*Barbara J. Yoder*
Lead apostle and author, Shekinah Regional Apostolic Center
Breakthrough Apostolic Ministries Network
Ann Arbor, Michigan

"Joshua Mills's ministry is so rich, manifesting the power of God's love for people. His life is full of spiritual fruit, and he moves in the realms of God's glory. Signs and wonders follow as he ministers. When I recently had the great honor to work with him, I observed his sensitivity to the voice and guidance of the Holy Spirit. I saw firsthand how the Spirit speaks to him and how He is obedient to act on the orders he receives from heaven. This book will be a true blessing to you as you learn to enter more deeply into God's presence."

—*Dr. Mary K. Baxter*
Best-selling author, Divine Revelation Series, including
*A Divine Revelation of Hell* and *A Divine Revelation of Heaven*

"The third reformation is marked by the rising up of the Third Day Church, moving in the fullness of God's glory, tasting of the goodness of His Word, and operating in the powers of the age to come! This book will be a powerful launching pad for all believers to be catapulted into the realms of faith, anointing, and glory that are so essential to thriving in the end times. I have personally witnessed Joshua ministering in these realms, and this book will be a gem for all workers of the kingdom in the day of His power!"

—*Chee Kang Seng*
Founder/Apostolic Overseer, Revive Asia
Living Streams International
Bangkok, Thailand

"As you read this book, expect to be caught up in the accelerating wheels of glory that are turning as new realms are opened unto you. We are living in days of supernatural acceleration, and I believe that this book contains understanding that will help bring the body of Christ into divine alignment with God's end-time purposes. Joshua Mills writes with words that will resonate within you and unleash revival in a greater way. The coming of Jesus will bring bright glory to everyone He touches, and this book foreshadows that truth."

—*Mary Hudson*
Arise International/Keith Hudson Ministries
Santa Barbara, California

"I'm really excited about this book, which explores the various realms of glory that we can freely explore as the people of God in this age of grace. If there is anyone in the world who knows how to lead us into these realms, it is Joshua Mills. I deeply love and admire this man of extraordinary spirituality and integrity, and I have witnessed first-hand the amazing glory realms that are being released through his life here on earth. This book will definitely change your walk with God forever."

—*Dr. Georg Karl*
Glory Life Network
Glory Harvest International Ministries
Stuttgart, Germany

"No one I know operates out of the glory realm like Joshua Mills. We have had the privilege of hosting Joshua a number of times at our conferences in New Zealand. Each time, there have been visible and tangible demonstrations of the glory—signs, wonders, and miracles. Joshua Mills is the real deal and walks in what he has written. For those who are hungry for the glory, this book is a must. It will definitely take you to higher realms!"

—*Tim Stevenson*
Senior Pastor, Horizon Church
Auckland, New Zealand

"Joshua Mills has paid a price in the presence of Jesus that is both inviting and provoking. His value for worship in the secret place is a treasure. His life and writings articulate truths that few others have tasted. I celebrate Joshua's life and ministry, and I honor his relentless focus on the glory of God, which is found in the face of Jesus. I know that *Moving in Glory Realms* will bless you greatly."

—*Michael Koulianos*
Founder, Jesus Image
Lake Mary, Florida

"Several years ago, I was radically impacted by Joshua Mills's ministry in Hong Kong. Subsequently, we've had him minister in our church near Durban, South Africa, and the impact on our fellowship has been tremendous. The sweetness of Jesus flows off of Joshua's life. He is the real deal—on and off the stage! This a must read for people who aren't content to only hear about the glory, but for those who want to experience the glory for themselves."

—*Steve Wheeler*
Senior Pastor, Highway Christian Church
Author, *Highway to Grace*
Pinetown, South Africa

"We were blessed to meet Joshua Mills when we had just started in ministry, and from our very first encounter, we learned so much from him. His humility, simplicity, and wisdom place him in a league of his own. This initial encounter caused us to dive into the glory realms that Joshua so generously imparted. His glory teachings converted into exponential increase in the supernatural, causing 'performance' to yield and 'rest' to increase—a powerful combination of both glory and grace that built us up and prepared us to move in a new dimension. Soon, what we had received from Joshua so freely, we now were able to impart with demonstration to our own church—tremendous signs and wonders followed and continue to this day. We are so thankful for Joshua and Janet's ministry, and we are honored to call them friends. We are excited to recommend this anointed book to all who hunger and thirst to experience the greatness of God."

—*Kirby & Fiona de Lanerolle*
Founders and overseers, WOW Life Ministries
Apostolic Diocese of Ceylon
Colombo, Sri Lanka

"Joshua Mills introduced the Inuit people to the supernatural realm, where entire communities have been greatly impacted with signs and wonders. Encouragingly, Joshua's grounded instructions demystify the mysteries of heaven, equipping readers to venture into glory realms."

—James Arreak
Founder, Iqaluit Christian Fellowship
Iqaluit, Nunavut, Canada

"The realms of glory are a place of transition and change. God deposits His life, love, and directions in new ways. *Moving in Glory Realms*, by Joshua Mills, will help you to enter into these greater dimensions of God."

—Dr. Jane Lowder
Director, Calvary Pentecostal Campground
Ashland, Virginia

"My friend Joshua Mills and I both want to adventure to Antarctica, because it is the only continent we have yet to visit. Similarly, we are both passionate about exploring the "final frontier" of *Moving in Glory Realms*! While most of our natural world has already been charted, there still remains an extraordinary world just waiting for us to discover—the spiritual world of the kingdom within. Joshua is our fearless leader, pioneering this holy dimension and showing us the way forward. His insight on the vibrational frequency of music creating an atmosphere for miracles and healing our bodies is profound. His exciting interactions with the angelic realm are biblical and his clear teaching on how to move from faith to anointing to glory is a true gift to the body of Christ. *Moving in Glory Realms* is what we were created for. Let the journey begin!"

—Dr. Charity Virkler Kayembe
Glory Waves Ministries
Coauthor, *Hearing God Through Your Dreams* and *Everyday Angels*

"Joshua Mills has a deep understanding of God's realms of glory, which he carries and releases across the world. At our church, we've received a powerful impartation of this each time Joshua has ministered here. Today, there is such a need for the church to experience and encounter the glory of God. In *Moving in Glory Realms*, Joshua shares many of the valuable keys that he has learned from his radical pursuit of the heart of God. Read it, and let the Holy Spirit catch you up into God's glory. I strongly recommend it to all those seeking His glory in their lives."

*—Phil Whitehead*
Senior Pastor, Chiswick Christian Centre
London, UK

"I love the teaching of Joshua Mills on the three spiritual realms. I have seen how the glory realm manifests on Joshua while he has ministered in our churches in Japan. This book shows us that there is a realm of glory where God's invisible realm becomes visible. God wants us to know His manifest presence like never before, because He will fill the whole earth with the knowledge of His glory. This is the book that will help us bring the glory of God in our lives!"

*—Gaius and Jaycie Lawrence*
Senior Leaders, Church of Praise International
Osaka, Japan

# MOVING *IN* GLORY REALMS

# MOVING IN GLORY REALMS

EXPLORING DIMENSIONS OF DIVINE PRESENCE

# JOSHUA MILLS

WHITAKER
HOUSE

Scripture quotations marked (NIV) are taken from the *Holy Bible, New International Version*®, NIV®, © 1973, 1978, 1984, 2011 by Biblica, Inc.® Used by permission of Zondervan. All rights reserved worldwide. www.zondervan.com. The "NIV" and "New International Version" are trademarks registered in the United States Patent and Trademark Office by Biblica, Inc.® Scripture quotations marked (KJV) are taken from the King James Version of the Holy Bible. Scripture quotations marked (KJVA) are taken from the King James Version of the Holy Bible with the Apocrypha. Scripture quotations marked (AMPC) are taken from *The Amplified*® *Bible, Classic Edition* © 1954, 1958, 1962, 1964, 1965, 1987 by The Lockman Foundation. Used by permission (www.Lockman.org). All rights reserved. Scripture quotations marked (ESV) are taken from *The Holy Bible, English Standard Version*, © 2000, 2001, 1995 by Crossway Bibles, a division of Good News Publishers. Used by permission. All rights reserved. Scripture quotations marked (NASB) are taken from the updated *New American Standard Bible*®, NASB®, © 1960, 1962, 1963, 1968, 1971, 1972, 1973, 1975, 1977, 1995 by The Lockman Foundation. Used by permission. (www.Lockman.org). Scripture quotations marked (MSG) are taken from *The Message: The Bible in Contemporary Language* by Eugene H. Peterson, © 1993, 1994, 1995, 1996, 2000, 2001, 2002. Used by permission of NavPress Publishing Group. All rights reserved. Represented by Tyndale House Publishers, Inc. Scripture quotation marked (ISV) is taken from the Holy Bible: International Standard Version®, © 1996-forever by The ISV Foundation. All rights reserved. Used by permission. Scripture quotations marked (NLT) are taken from the *Holy Bible, New Living Translation*, © 1996, 2004, 2007 by Tyndale House Foundation. Used by permission of Tyndale House Publishers, Inc., Carol Stream, Illinois 60188. All rights reserved. Scripture quotation marked (BLB) is taken from *The Holy Bible, Berean Study Bible*, BSB, copyright © 2016 by Bible Hub. Used by Permission. All Rights Reserved Worldwide.

Unless otherwise indicated, dictionary definitions are taken from *Dictionary.com Unabridged*. Random House, Inc.

Greek and Hebrew word definitions are taken from *Strong's Exhaustive Concordance of the Bible*.

Boldface type in the Scripture quotations indicates the author's emphasis.

Graphic designs by Ken Vail.

## MOVING IN GLORY REALMS:
### Exploring Dimensions of Divine Presence

International Glory Ministries
P.O. Box 4037
Palm Springs, CA 92263
JoshuaMills.com
info@joshuamills.com

ISBN: 978-1-64123-086-5
eBook ISBN: 978-1-64123-087-2
Printed in the United States of America
© 2018 by Joshua Mills

Whitaker House
1030 Hunt Valley Circle
New Kensington, PA 15068
www.whitakerhouse.com

Library of Congress Cataloging-in-Publication Data (Pending)

No part of this book may be reproduced or transmitted in any form or by any means, electronic or mechanical—including photocopying, recording, or by any information storage and retrieval system—without permission in writing from the publisher. Please direct your inquiries to permissionseditor@whitakerhouse.com.

1 2 3 4 5 6 7 8 9 10 11 **ᒪᒧ** 25 24 23 22 21 20 19 18

# DEDICATION

This book is dedicated to every seeker who has oftentimes felt misunderstood or spiritually blocked, and yet, still has a longing to go deeper in the things of God. I see you; I feel you; I bless your journey. The door is open for you here. Look up! Go forward! You have permission to explore the depths of new territories in the liberty of the Spirit. You're invited to join me in *Moving in Glory Realms*.

# ACKNOWLEDGMENTS

There are so many people whom God has used to bless, guide, and influence my life and make this book possible. Here are just a few:

Ruth and Frances, thank you for thrusting this project forward in the most extraordinary way.

My wife, Janet, and my children: Lincoln, Liberty and Legacy. I could've never written this book without your undivided support and sacrificial devotion to the glory. I love you.

My parents, Ron and Nancy Mills, and my father-in-law, John Bechard, for always encouraging and supporting the work of God in my life, even when it wasn't fully understandable at the time.

Special thanks to Melanie Hart (personal assistant), Harold McDougal (editor), Jean Albright (transcriptions), Don Milam, Bob Whitaker, and the entire team at Whitaker House.

So many others who have stood, supported, and worked alongside this revelation: Pam and Shelly Couch, Billie Deck, Jodi Fecera, Heidi Gillcrist, Ed and Nina Honorat, Catherine Keron, Linda Koenig, Sonny and Marylou Morgan, D. Karl and Cheryl Thomas, Bill and Beverly Wilson, and Tom and Jeannette Wuhrman.

And Susie Rainer, for offering me a "secret place" to rest, revelate, and write.

I must also thank every pastor and ministry that has warmly welcomed me into their congregations over the past twenty years. The writing of this book is a result of the glorious encounters that we've shared together. I'm forever grateful.

# CONTENTS

# FOREWORD

In every generation, there is a company of people who have experienced God in brand new ways. Emerging from those experiences is a new voice, exhibiting and declaring the character of God. It has been my pleasure to become friends with many in this new tribe of anointed men and women.

Joshua Mills is one of the more highly respected members of that anointed company. He has unusual favor on his life, as well as incredible insight into the purposes and nature of God. Some in this group are great speakers, but not gifted writers. Some are great writers but not gifted teachers. Then there are those who are able to do both well. Joshua is one of those: a gifted communicator and a gifted writer.

In his new book, *Moving in Glory Realms*, he touches on a subject that is close to my heart—the glory of God. Though there have been many sermons preached and many books written on this subject, Joshua brings fresh insight to the nature of God's glory. His book offers impassioned theological insight into this subject. But it is more than a teaching book. Joshua has lived in that glory realm, and he has filled his book with stories from that realm. It would be nearly impossible to not be encouraged and challenged to start your own personal journey into the glory in reading this book.

Joshua is determined to enter more and more deeply into the glory of God. He understands that in the glory, there is increase, there is abundance, there is healing, there is life, there is wholeness, there is provision, there is prosperity, and there is deliverance.

I agree with Joshua when he writes these words, "As you begin to navigate within the glory realm, you will hear things you have never heard before and see things you have never seen before."

He has discovered that there are realms within the spiritual dimension that cooperatively move together in unison to bring forth the greater purposes of God on the earth.

He truly is a pioneer and is discovering that the deeper you go into the glory, the deeper the glory will go into you. As you give yourself more fully to this realm, suddenly you will find yourself thinking of the glory, speaking about the glory, and moving in the glory.

We live in times when darkness covers much of the earth. But the glory of God upon His people is becoming more and more realized, casting out darkness, bringing hope to the most hopeless situations.

The heart to seek God is birthed in us by God Himself. Like all desires, it is not something that can be demanded or forced. Instead, it grows within us as we become exposed to the nature of God. He creates in us an appetite for Himself by lavishing us with the reality of His goodness—His irresistible glory. As we behold His glory in the midst of mystery, He will transform our perception and increase our faith and freedom in who He is!

I encourage you to read Joshua's book, not only to learn about the glory but to be changed by the glory. It is a book I highly recommend. But not just so you can learn principles about the glory. My desire is for all of us to be transformed by the glory. I expect that to be the outcome of reading *Moving in Glory Realms*.

—*Bill Johnson*
Senior Leader, Bethel Church, Redding, CA
Author, *Hosting the Presence* and *God Is Good*

# DEFINITIONS

**ATMOSPHERE**: "A surrounding or pervading mood, environment, or influence." When I speak of creating, maintaining, or occupying an atmosphere, it means to spiritually cultivate an environment that is conducive for the influence of heaven to affect our spirit, soul, and physical well-being.

**DIMENSION**: "Measurement in length, width, and thickness," also "scope; importance." Dimensions in the Spirit can be measured in length, width, and breadth as degrees or levels of spiritual authority.

**GLORY**: The glory is the complete person of God (Father, Son, and Spirit), and is also the place of His heavenly abode. Where He is, heaven is. The glory is the goodness, the fullness, the splendor, and the awareness of His manifest presence.

**GOLDEN GLORY**: A term used for the manifestation of *shekinah* glory that visibly appears in physical form, most often as small dust-like particles. It usually has a golden sheen in appearance, but can also present itself in other colors or with a crystal-clear glimmer. Most notably, this physical manifestation generally appears coming up through the pores of the skin, but at other times can also fall through the atmosphere.

**PRAISE**: "The act of expressing approval or admiration; commendation; laudation. The offering of grateful homage in words or song." Praise is acknowledging God for what He has done, what He is doing, and what He will do. It is a faith act that must precede the act of worship. Praise is often accompanied by dancing, shouting, and corporate celebratory music.

**REALM**: "The region, sphere, or domain within which anything occurs, prevails, or dominates." There are three specific spiritual realms: faith, anointing, and glory. Each realm contains a dominant theme and specific protocol for access. When speaking of the glory realm, this is the domain or kingdom of God that contains the fullness of God and all heavenly realities.

**SPHERE**: "The place or environment within which a person or thing exists; a field of activity or operation." There are many spheres within realms. Each sphere has its own limitations, operations, and boundaries, but each one can become a gateway to a greater sphere.

**WORSHIP**: "Reverent honor and homage paid to God or a sacred personage, or to any object regarded as sacred. Formal or ceremonious rendering of such honor and homage. Adoring reverence or regard." Worship is acknowledging God for who He is. It is the act of bowing down to reverence His majesty and the spiritual progression from praise.

*He measured off a thousand cubits and then led me through water that was ankle-deep. He measured off another thousand cubits and led me through water that was knee-deep. He measured off another thousand and led me through water that was up to the waist. He measured off another thousand, but now it was a river that I could not cross, because the water had risen and was deep enough to swim in—a river that no one could cross.*
—Ezekiel 47:3–5

# INTRODUCTION

*Wherever the spirit would go, they would go,*
*and the wheels would rise along with them,*
*because the spirit of the living creatures was in the wheels.*
—Ezekiel 1:20

**J**ust like wheels within wheels that are moving and accelerating, there are realms within the spiritual dimension that cooperatively move together in unison to bring forth the greater purposes of God. These are realms within realms.

In our own lives, and throughout the Scriptures, we see God working in threes. The Father, Son, and Holy Spirit, in divine collaboration, are inviting us into salvation, baptism, and the manifest presence of glory. The number three gives us a picture of completeness, as it is the first spiritually perfect number. In speaking of the death, burial, and resurrection of our Lord, we're given a prophetic understanding of the first-day, the second-day, and the third-day church arising in the kingdom, the power, and the glory. Jesus arose, conquering death, hell, and the grave on the third day, after ministering for three years here on the earth, and, at the time, He was only thirty-three years old. Jesus Christ is the same yesterday, today, and forever, and He is the way, the truth, and the life.

In terms of the blessing, it was passed on through the lineage of Abraham, Isaac, and Jacob. In the life of a believer, we are given the tri-fold opportunity to manifest a thirty-fold, a sixty-fold, and a hundred-fold multiplication, with the command to become witnesses in Jerusalem, Judea, and Samaria (including the outermost parts of the earth). So, you can see that God works in threes. There are also three realms in the Spirit.

The first of these realms is the realm of faith. The second is the realm of the anointing. The anointing is different from faith, and faith is different from the anointing. The third realm of the Spirit is the realm of the glory. This is the realm into which the Spirit is leading us. Ezekiel had a vision of the river flowing from the temple and was introduced to its flowing waters step by step. I've discovered that we don't necessarily come into the things of God all at once. We may suddenly experience something glorious, but the reality is that the Spirit of truth is leading us on a journey.

Don't become discouraged by your lack of experience in God. Revelation is always progressive. In the same way that Ezekiel experienced the river by first dipping his feet into the water up to his ankles, God will do that for each one of us in the area of faith. As we continue to walk humbly before the Lord with a teachable spirit, He introduces us to the waters that are knee- deep. At this level, we begin to understand the realm of anointing that comes with greater power, but we cannot disregard our initial experiences, or the experiences of those who still stand in the shallow waters. Instead, we know that if it had not been for those waters, we would not be able to experience the greater depths.

Everything in God leads to something greater. Even our salvation experience in Christ is not the end-all, but rather the opening of new horizons for spiritual exploration under the protection of His blood and the doorway of the cross. In Him we live, and move, and have our being.

There is always a moving in the Spirit. We go from the realms of faith to anointing, from ankle-deep to knee-deep waters, and yet Ezekiel was led to the waters that were at his waist. In this realm, we are introduced to the glory of God. And yet, again, this is just the beginning.

Once we begin to touch the glory, we discover that there are realms within that realm. We are swept into the depths of the Spirit, in waters that are over our heads. This is a realm we can swim in. It's a realm we can live in. If we want to experience the fullness of God in all of

His supernatural goodness, we must understand the three realms of the Spirit. Then, as we begin to understand these three realms, we can accelerate through them. Each realm is a portal into something greater as they interact with each other. Once you comprehend this dynamic of the Spirit, you'll quickly move within the glory.

In the same way there are three realms in the Spirit, there are also three dimensions within mankind. The first dimension is the spirit-man. The second dimension is the soul. Yes, there is an absolute distinction between our spirit and our soul because the Scriptures say, *"The word of God is living and active. Sharper than any double-edged sword, it penetrates even to dividing soul and spirit, joints and marrow; it judges the thoughts and attitudes of the heart"* (Hebrews 4:12). Our spirit is located within what the Word calls our heart. (See Romans 10:9; 1 Peter 3:4.) Our soul is comprised of our mind, our will, and our emotions.

The third dimension within mankind is the physical body. We are made spirit, soul, and body. It is mistakenly said, "We are body, soul, and spirit," but the essence of who we are is not a body. Our body is simply an *earthsuit* for who we are and who God created us to be. We are a spirit-being that has a soul but lives in a physical body.

Interestingly enough, the three dimensions of mankind respond to the three realms in the Spirit. The first dimension of mankind, the spirit-man, responds to the realm of faith. Your spirit-man is the initial point of contact for any interaction with the Spirit realm. When God brings the revelation of salvation to our lives, it is our spirit-man that reaches out in faith to receive it. We cannot receive the blessings of God in bodily form until we have first received them in our spirit-man.

The impartation of God always comes first in the Spirit before it manifests physically. That's why our spirit-man dimension corresponds with the realm of faith. On the other hand, our soul (mind, will, and emotions) is the dimension that responds to the realm of the anointing. In the anointing, our soul dimension is activated. Often in the anointing, you feel something, and your emotions are at an all-time high. It's not uncommon for people to laugh or cry or feel great comfort, healing, or excitement when the anointing touches them.

When we encounter the realm of the anointing, therefore, it connects with our soul dimension, and we feel an awareness of the Spirit, the heat of God, or the electricity of His power, and we must worship. Feeling things in the anointing happens in our soul realm. Even though feelings first appear in the soul realm, they are a result of what has been imparted to our spirit-man. What begins in the Spirit flows from our spirit-man, into our soul, and, finally, into our physical body. It is in our bodies that we respond to the realm of the glory.

We see an example of this at the dedication of Solomon's temple. (See 2 Chronicles 5:13–14.) The people of Israel were praising and worshiping God, when the cloud of His glory descended upon them, the fire of God consumed the sacrifice, and the smoke of His glory filled the atmosphere. It was such a powerful encounter that the ministers (the priests in this case) could not perform their service. In other words, they couldn't do what they normally did. Why? Because their bodies were responding to the weight of God's magnificent glory. This explains why many people experience feeling a strong vibration, a numbness, a shaking, or even fall down in the atmosphere of manifest glory. Their flesh has begun to yield to the glory of God. When our flesh falls down, our spirit rises up in strength.

In the glory, God does for us what we cannot do for ourselves. During the late nineties, God gave us three signs to help bring understanding to what He was teaching us. The first sign was the supernatural fragrance of heaven. When heaven appeared in the meetings, it couldn't be seen, yet was fully present. By faith we received this sign.

The second sign was the supernatural oil. It dripped from the heads and hands of those whom the Lord chose. Interestingly, the supernatural oil also carried the fragrance of heaven, and we understood that God was anointing us.

The third sign that appeared was the golden glory. During times of worship, tiny sparkles of dust-like particles shimmered on our skin, on our clothing, and in our Bibles. It happened in a corporate way among our church members, and we recognized that God was calling us together into His glory. This golden glory, like the manna of Moses's day, cannot be fully understood. It seems to be a newly created substance with an unknown molecular structure. When tested, it was found to have an oily substance within it.[1] Throughout the Scriptures, gold represents the glory of God, and we discerned that was where He was leading us.

The result of those initial experiences with the glory has been a lifetime spent traveling to more than seventy-five nations of the world and ministering to hundreds of thousands (if not millions) of people. Many were changed, transformed by this message of the glory. We have witnessed some of the most spectacular healings and extraordinary miracles while living in these glory realms.

At times, we have even been caught up within the whirlwind of God and transported in the Spirit to other places, to gain supernatural insight and minister to others by divine revelation. We've tapped into a place in God where provision and abundance flow without resistance. Money miracles and angelic assistance have become the norm with us.

Now, through the pages of this book, I share these experiences with you and build for you a foundational framework so that you, too, can move in the glory with ease. It is essential that you read through the entire book, little by little, allowing God to lead you, step by step. Each realm builds upon the one before. In the process, God builds and establishes something inside of each of us as we move from faith to faith, strength to strength, and glory to glory.

As you read, allow time for the Spirit to minister to you directly with an inflow of anointing that brings a deeper awareness of His presence. God takes us from faith to anointing to glory. Are you ready to begin moving with me into these exciting *Glory Realms*?

# PART I
# MOVING IN THE SPIRIT

*For in him we live and move and have our being.*
—Acts 17:28

# 1

# REALMS OF FAITH

*For in it the righteousness of God is revealed from faith to faith;*
*as it is written, "But the righteous man shall live by faith."*
—Romans 1:17 NASB

**E**verybody has faith! This might not seem like a revelation but consider the fact that many people complain about not having any faith at all. The Scriptures tell us that God gave a measure of faith to each and every individual. (See Romans 12:3.) This means even atheists and agnostics have faith of some sort. Yes, they do! But their faith is rooted in humanistic theories, scientific studies, and man-made technologies. They trust their own minds. As spiritual people, we know this is foolish, because: *"Those who trust in themselves are fools, but those who walk in wisdom are kept safe"* (Proverbs 28:26). *"Trust in the LORD with all your heart and lean not on your own understanding"* (Proverbs 3:5). The kind of faith that is pleasing to God is God-faith, and we can learn how to grow in this realm.

In the early days of our ministry, our sphere of influence was mostly local and regional (extending within a two-hour driving radius from where we lived in London, Ontario, Canada). We drove to our ministry engagements and often took a team with us. Little by little, others heard about what God was doing in our lives. In this way, God opened the door for us to extend our ministry outreach farther afield. Then, a pastor in Seattle, Washington, called and asked if I would come and minister for a New Year's prophetic weekend that his church was hosting. It was a small church and unable to cover my airfare expense, but they had a great desire to see God move in His glory through our ministry.

At this point in our lives, we had faith to trust God for the finances to put gas in our car, but, hadn't yet learned how to stretch our faith for airline tickets. But I've discovered that when God wants to take us into a higher dimension of supernatural living, He invites us into a place of being stretched. Driving all the way to Seattle on my own would be too much. Then we learned there was a bus service that could take me across the country, and we had faith for the bus ticket. So, we prayed. Within days, God brought the money to meet our immediate point of need.

That bus ride to Seattle took four long days, days without a shower, a clean bathroom, or any place to get a decent meal. But I can tell you that through this situation, God began developing my faith. I was being stretched—physically, emotionally, and spiritually—on that trip. I quickly realized if we were called to the nations, we needed a better way to travel, and that required an increase of faith.

Faith gives birth to greater faith. That bus ticket was my faith seed. God received that little seed and used it in a marvelous way. On the last night of ministry in Seattle, a gentleman who was attending the meetings approached me. The weight of glory we experienced in the corporate atmosphere had deeply touched him. He asked what airline I had flown to get there. When I told him I hadn't come on a plane but traveled four days on a bus, he was astonished. Later that evening, I received a phone call from him at the place where I was staying. It was so long ago that I can't remember exactly how it all happened. But what I do remember is that he decided to bless me with a first-class airplane ticket for the remainder of my ministry tour. (I had been scheduled to travel by bus next to San Diego, California, then the long trip back to eastern Canada.) He used my small faith, the seemingly insignificant seed that I sowed, to bring forth something greater. For me, the Lord taking my bus fare and turning it into a first-class airplane ticket was just as miraculous as Jesus turning water into wine. He moves us from faith to faith.

In the Scriptures, our faith is likened to a mustard seed, small but spicy. (See Matthew 17:20.) The seeds of faith we sow today will bring us a harvest of greater faith for tomorrow. Jesus told a parable about a little mustard seed that was planted and became the greatest among all the garden plants, substantial enough to provide shade and safety for birds that lodged under the shadow of it. (See Mark 4:31–32.) Don't be afraid to take your small steps of faith now, as insignificant as they might seem to you in the moment. Trust that God is able to make those small steps count for something considerable in the long term. Because He leads and guides us, our small beginning steps will lead to great discoveries. Our faith walk is a journey into securing our heavenly purpose.

## WE MUST BEGIN WITH FAITH

In order to enter into the fullness of God's glory, we begin in the area of faith. Faith is the starting point for all spiritual experiences. The moment you stop moving in faith, you no longer move in the Spirit. Every other realm in the Spirit is established and functions on the foundation of faith. The writer of Hebrews tells us that we cannot please God without it. (See Hebrews 11:6.) The basis for our sacred pilgrimage must be the discovery of who God is and what He does, and that requires faith.

## THE IDENTITY OF FAITH

As a young child, growing up in a Christian home, I heard the word *faith* often. It was even the name of our church. This word was used so much that I never took much time to think about what it actually meant. It wasn't until I was older that I discovered how powerful faith really is.

According to the dictionary, *faith* is "the belief and trust in and loyalty to God," including "firm belief in something for which there is no proof."[1] For most people, this may seem irrational, but in the realm of the Spirit, it is the only way to operate successfully. Faith is the supernatural bridge between the *now* and the *not yet*. It is the spiritual force that pulls the future promises of God into our here-and-now reality.

> FAITH IS THE SUPERNATURAL BRIDGE BETWEEN THE *NOW* AND THE *NOT YET*. IT IS THE SPIRITUAL FORCE THAT PULLS THE FUTURE PROMISES OF GOD INTO OUR HERE-AND-NOW REALITY.

In Hebrews 11:1, the Bible declares, *"Now faith is."* Faith is now. It is always in the now. We need to speak in the now and receive in the now because this is the place where faith resides. Faith is not in the future, and it hasn't passed away. We need to stop putting all our hope in some other time frame. Faith grabs hold of the covenant promises of God and delivers them in the now.

Have you ever heard people say, "Maybe I'll get my miracle tomorrow"? "Maybe this (or that) will happen tomorrow"? Even in church meetings, ministers have said, "You may not get your miracle today, but come back Sunday night, and you'll get it." We have this habit of putting the best things of God into the future. Every time we take a step forward, our miracle takes a step forward as well. It's always another week's delay, another month's delay, or another year's delay. But God wants to give us now faith, because He is a now God. The One who was, who is, and who is to come is present among us right now. Faith receives the now of God, and in that now is the new.

## NEW SPIRITUAL FOUNDATIONS

When God is about to do something new, He lays new spiritual foundations, because you can't put new wine into old wineskins. You cannot put the new move of the Spirit into old traditions, habits, religious rites, ideas, or mindsets. Paul said, *"According to the grace of God which is given unto me, as a wise masterbuilder, I have laid the foundation, and another buildeth thereon. But let every man take heed how he buildeth thereupon"* (1 Corinthians 3:10 KJV). A new foundation is being laid.

Faith is the foundation for every other realm in the Spirit, so we need to be careful how we build on this foundation. You cannot put something stale with something fresh because it spoils the freshness of it. By faith we obtain access into new (to us) and greater realms in the Spirit.

Hebrews 11:1 tells us that faith is both spiritual *substance* and spiritual *evidence*. The dictionary defines *substance* as "the ultimate reality that underlies all outward manifestations and change," also "physical material from which something is made or which has discrete existence."[2] In essence, faith is the foundational reality that underlies all outward manifestations and the spiritual material from which all outcomes are made. *Evidence* is "an outward sign or indication, something that furnishes proof as testimony or one who bears witness." We utilize the substance of our faith to produce the evidence for it.

## THE THREE DIMENSIONS OF FAITH

Scripture speaks of the process of being changed as we go from faith to faith. This gives us an understanding of the progressive momentum in the Spirit. Spiritually speaking, we are strengthened inwardly even as we are being led from one dimension of trusting God to the next.

In the same way that there are three realms in the Spirit, there are also three dimensions of faith within that realm, and at times they overlap. Some of us are guilty of hanging around the lower dimensions of faith and not exercising the spiritual muscle God has given us.

### LITTLE FAITH

Jesus spoke about *"little faith."* (See Matthew 8:26; Luke 12:28.) This is the natural faith we all possess to trust in anything at all. Many trust in themselves or the government, insurance plans, and health-care systems. This is called little faith or weak faith because it relies on everything and everybody except God.

### GREAT FAITH

When we hear and receive the truths of the Scriptures and our spirit enlarges, we are brought to another dimension of faith. This is what is called *great faith*. (See Matthew 8:10; Matthew 15:21–28.) This faith believes in God, trusts in His Word and His power, and presents itself to Him to receive (by faith) what it needs. The centurion of Matthew 8:5–13 was said to have great faith. He believed the healing word spoken by Jesus could, by itself, bring a cure to his servant who had a leprous condition. Jesus was impressed by this passionate pursuit of divine healing, stating that He had never found such great faith anywhere else.

The woman with the issue of blood in Scripture also had great faith. (See Matthew 9:20–22; Mark 5:25–34; Luke 8:43–48.) Despite her physical agony, this faith caused her to press through the crowd in order to touch the hem of the garment of the Miracle Worker. When she made the divine connection, Jesus felt healing virtue flow from His body into hers. In a revelatory moment of response, He told her that *her* faith had made her whole. It wasn't Jesus's faith that worked the miracle; it was this woman's faith.

Great faith belongs to *you*; it is *your* faith in action. I want you to understand this. Great faith is your responsibility. You are able to release it where and when you need it. In this sphere Jesus said, *"According to your faith be it unto you"* (Matthew 9:29 KJV).

## PERFECT FAITH

There is another dimension of faith available for the believer in which to operate. This is the highest level of faith called *perfect faith*. (See John 5:30; James 1:6; James 2:22.) While Jesus was on the earth, He walked in this perfect dimension of faith influence. He spoke, transacted, was directed by, and functioned under the understanding of God's perfect will and methods of divine operation. As a result, He only did what He saw the Father doing—nothing more and nothing less. He only said what He heard the Father speaking—not adding or taking away a single word.

FAITH *IN* GOD BELIEVES THE MIRACULOUS IS ACCESSIBLE WHEN AND HOW GOD PERMITS, BUT THE FAITH *OF* GOD UNDERSTANDS THE NEW COVENANT BY DIVINE REVELATION AND KNOWS THAT THE MIRACLE IS AVAILABLE NOW.

Perfect faith is the actual faith *of* God, not faith *from* God. It is in this place of faith that we can say, *"In him we live, and move and have our being"* (Acts 17:28). Many believers have faith in God, but they don't have the faith of God. This is why many suffer lack in spirit, soul, and body.

There is a world of difference between these two types of faith. Faith in God relies on our understanding. Our faith input determines our miracle output. Faith in God believes the miraculous is accessible when and how God permits, but the faith *of* God understands the new covenant by divine revelation and knows that the miracle is available now. The faith *of* God relies on the Spirit's ability alone. Faith imparted to us by the Spirit is perfect, permanent, and cannot be swayed. This faith that Jesus had is available for us today.

Paul wrote,

*I have been crucified with Christ, and I no longer live, but Christ lives in me. And that which I now live in the flesh, I live through faith from the Son of God, the One having loved me and having given up Himself for me.*                    (Galatians 2:20 BLB)

The King James Version of the Bible calls it, *"the faith of the Son of God."* The apostle Paul was speaking about this supernatural faith of God that is divinely given to us. Perfect faith enables us to always overcome, and opens up the floodgates for a deluge of anointing. This faith doesn't come from self-effort or positive confession, but from the Spirit.

The faith of God is what the writer of Hebrews was speaking about when he said, *"By faith we understand that the universe was formed at God's command, so that what is seen was not made out of what was visible"* (Hebrews 11:3). It was in this realm of faith that everything came into being in the beginning. The faith of God can only come by supernatural infusion and will synchronize our steps in the Spirit as the Word of God becomes the power of God living inside of us.

There are significant differences between these three faith dimensions. As we progress in the Spirit, we should accelerate through them. As you exercise your faith more, and walk in it more, your spiritual senses become heightened and intensely alert. Exploring the dimensions of faith activates your spiritual senses so you can perceive what is taking place, even when others are unaware of it.

Faith also takes on many different expressions, each with their own personality and attitude. Faith hears and sees and speaks and tastes. Faith also either receives or refuses. Most importantly, faith takes action!

## HAVING EARS TO HEAR

Paul wrote to the Roman believers, *"So faith comes from hearing, and hearing through the word of Christ"* (Romans 10:17 ESV). Faith hears. What does it hear? Faith hears the Word, which is spirit and life (see John 6:63), and increases according to its supernatural inflow. Faith hears both the spoken prophetic *rhema* word, as well as the *logos* Word of God.

At the close of many of Jesus's significant exhortations, He used the phrase, *"Whoever has ears, let them hear."*(See Matthew 11:15; Matthew 13:9; Mark 4:9, 23; Mark 8:18; Luke 14:35.) John also mentioned it several times in Revelation. (See Revelation 2:7, 11, 17, 29; 3: 6, 13, 22; 13:9.) These verses show us the importance of giving ourselves fully to the things of the Spirit in order to receive the spiritual benefit.

The Greek word *logos* literally means "the universal, divine reason or mind of God."[3] When your ears are open to hear God's Word by faith, an infusion of God's mind and divine reason are imparted to your spirit. The Word of God is *"the power of God"* (Romans 1:16). One of the greatest things you can do is be around people, places, and atmospheres that continually speak the Word. Your ears will hear it, and your spirit will respond with accelerated increase because of it.

When your ears are opened by faith, get ready to listen to the unseen realm. Faith creates doorways of possibility. It opens portals for the invisible realm to be made manifest in the natural.

Recently, while ministering at a four-day Glory School in Taipei, Taiwan, we heard the voices of heaven in the midst of our worship. On three separate occasions, as we sang in the Spirit, we noticed a sound that was above our sound. Voices sang continuously, without taking a breath. The angels of heaven had gathered around to join us in worshiping the Lord in song.

The first time I remember this happening in a corporate dynamic was when we were ministering at the Arctic Fall Bible Conference in Baker Lake, Nunavut, hosted by Pastor Joan Kashla. More than five hundred people gathered in the community arena to worship the Lord. As our singing intensified, the sound of angels singing "Holy,

Holy, Holy," resounded above our earthly voices. When we paused in that atmosphere of holiness, the song of the angels continued. It has always amazed me that angels don't need to take a breath when they sing. Their song of worship unto the Lord is constant, just as the worship in heaven is never-ending.

Many other times we have heard, through ears of faith, the sounds of heaven. Sometimes we've heard the heavenly instruments and choir, the song of the Lord, or the specific directives of His voice. Faith gives you ears to hear what you cannot hear in the natural.

## HAVING EYES TO SEE

Your faith also has eyes, and you must understand this truth. Faith is never blind; it never acts on impulse or whim. It sees, observes, and explores in the realm of the Spirit. In the same way that my physical eyes allow my mind to understand the natural world around me, my faith allows my spirit-man to understand the realm of the divine supernatural.

Rev. F. F. Bosworth, a depression-era faith healer, has been quoted as saying, "Faith begins where the will of God is known."[4] Faith transfers the blessings I see from the Spirit dimension into natural manifestation. You can't take hold of something if you've never seen it.

Faith sees the solution, not the problem. Faith sees the answer, not the question. Faith sees the miracle, not the mess. Your eyes must be open to see what God is doing. Faith gives you those eyes to see what God sees!

David had this kind of supernatural vision. Read Psalm 22, and you will realize that David's faith in God took him places in the Spirit and allowed him to see things that were yet to come to pass in the natural. He witnessed the crucifixion and resurrection of Jesus about a thousand years before they happened. (See Psalm 22:14–18; Acts 2:31–32.) At one point, as David lifted up his eyes, he saw an angel standing between earth and heaven. (See

> FAITH SEES THE SOLUTION, NOT THE PROBLEM. FAITH SEES THE ANSWER, NOT THE QUESTION. FAITH SEES THE MIRACLE, NOT THE MESS.

1 Chronicles 21:16.) Your faith gives you vision to see things you've never seen before. Abraham looked and then he believed. (See Genesis 15:5–6.)

Your faith also gives you the ability to see things before they've happened in the natural. This will strengthen your courage to reach out and receive them. Faith grabs hold of eternity and pulls the future into the present reality.

Several years ago, I preached on this subject in a meeting where the worship leader was Steve Swanson. He took the words of my revelation and wrote a song using them. The chorus says, "I'm pulling my future into now by the Spirit of God within. Earthly time is running out, and eternity's running in!"[5] You and I are approaching the end of the earthly timeline. As people of faith, we should expect to see an increased invasion of heavenly glory in the coming days.

As I mentioned in the Introduction, in the late 1990s, God gave us three supernatural signs—a heavenly fragrance that permeated our meetings, oil on our hands and other parts of our bodies, and the appearance of golden glory, which helped bring understanding to what He was teaching us. We needed eyes to see what God was saying. Too often, we don't watch with eyes of faith and, as a result, we miss the miracle right in front of us. Faith gives you eyes to see what God is doing and where He is leading.

## LEARNING TO SPEAK THE LANGUAGE OF FAITH

In the same way that faith hears and sees, it also has a voice that speaks with precision. Fear-filled words will defeat you, but faith-filled words will cause you to prosper. Words are the most powerful thing in the universe, containing the capacity for blessing and cursing. God wants to give you His now-words of faith. He wants to give you a word that's filled with total victory and copious blessing:

> *"The word is near you; it is in your mouth and in your heart," that is, the message concerning faith that we proclaim: If you declare with your mouth, "Jesus is Lord," and believe in your heart that God raised him from the dead, you will be saved.* (Romans 10:8–9)

Our words reveal the thoughts, intents, and beliefs that we carry within. When we receive the faith of God for an issue, our words change. That is what begins the supernatural shift in the natural realm. Faith boldly speaks the word that has the power to save.

I want you to get this into your spirit-man. At times, God will give you by faith a word in season that has the power to alter the course of history for an individual, a family, a region, or a nation. Many times when I've been in the middle of ministering, I say something revelatory that I had never thought of saying before. It came from the realm of the Spirit directly into my spirit, bypassing my head altogether. That's faith speaking.

At other times, I've found myself declaring accurate personal details, things impossible for me to know naturally, and future blessings over a person. There is no explanation for this, except that faith speaks at that moment. The prophetic unction works this way. Faith speaks about the promise as though already received, long before it is ever naturally felt, seen, or heard. We confess with our lips what we believe in our spirit. Faith speaks what it sees in the supernatural dimension. When the voice of faith speaks, vision is received.

Several years ago, I was caught up in the Spirit one night and taken high atop Huascaran, a mountain in the western Andes of Peru. I found myself praising and dancing atop that mountain all night long. By faith, my spirit sang over and over the truth of the Scripture, *"With joy you will draw water from the wells of salvation"* (Isaiah 12:3). I knew God was working through that word.

A few weeks later, Jim Drown, a great friend and evangelist, invited me to minister with him in Atlanta. He lives in Georgia but has a network of ministry in Peru. I told him that I couldn't go to Atlanta but could minister for him in Peru, because God had already spoken by faith through my spirit when I was high atop the mountain, giving me clarity of vision for the assignment at hand. All the arrangements

> WE CONFESS WITH OUR LIPS WHAT WE BELIEVE IN OUR SPIRIT. FAITH SPEAKS WHAT IT SEES IN THE SUPERNATURAL DIMENSION. WHEN THE VOICE OF FAITH SPEAKS, VISION IS RECEIVED.

were made. When we got to Lima, God confirmed His Word. We had a great harvest of souls in every meeting as the glory of God was ushered into the atmosphere.

Your words contain the power to create the world you'll walk in tomorrow. Your future is contained within the words that you speak today. Go into the heavens and listen to what God is saying. Listen for His words, see the pictures, images, and colors He displays. See what He's doing, then declare it. Speak it into the atmosphere by faith. Then watch Him confirm it for you.

For more than twenty years, I've been actively involved in ministry, traveling to many nations. As I have gone from place to place, God gave me His words to speak. I have declared revival and then saw it come to pass.

In Kangiqsujuaq, Nunavik, we witnessed every single resident of that entire community come to the saving knowledge of Jesus Christ. In other places, I declared miracles and saw them break out, sometimes thousands at one time. I love living and walking by faith because God leads, and faith speaks.

## FLAVORS OF FAITH

Earlier, I mentioned that faith was spicy like the mustard seed. Faith has a flavor able to overcome the bitterness of fear. When faith shows up, ungodly fear must exit. Faith also has the ability to taste the flavors of heaven. Several times in our meetings, when people experienced supernatural encounters with God manifesting His glory, they have tasted a sweet flavor. The Scriptures tell us that God's Word is sweet like honey. (See Ezekiel 3:3; Revelation 10:9–10.) Spiritually speaking, when revelation flows like honey in our meetings, people taste that reality. *"Taste and see that the LORD is good; blessed is the one who takes refuge in him"* (Psalm 34:8).

A young Australian lady who attended our meetings in Auckland, New Zealand, smelled and tasted an overwhelming flavor of toothpaste in her mouth. That night her teeth were supernaturally whitened in the atmosphere of glory. Excited, she shared her testimony with everyone in attendance.

This same thing has happened to many others as we spent time ministering in the Canadian Arctic. During one Easter conference in Kangirsuk, Nunavik,[6] many of the Inuit's teeth were whitened, some teeth straightened, and other people received gold and silver fillings. God does miracles in a way that may seem unusual to us, but I think it is wonderful. Faith not only hears, sees, and speaks. It also presses in to taste the goodness of God.

## FAITH REQUIRES ACTION

God's Word always prospers. If it is alive inside of you, you will also prosper. The faith of God moves you to action. You won't be able to stand still when God's Word becomes alive in you. Faith reaches out and takes hold of whatever grace provides.

James wrote, *"But be ye doers of the word, and not hearers only, deceiving your own selves"* (James 1:22 KJV), and *"For as the body without the spirit is dead, so faith without works is dead also"* (James 2:26 KJV). I have discovered that, in the Spirit, we are given a window of thirty to forty seconds to respond to His instructions. If we don't learn how to move immediately, we become lazy, distracted, or analytical about the instructions we have received.

When God speaks, we must listen. Delayed obedience is disobedience. Everything about this faith realm is contingent upon our willingness to respond. We must do what we say and say what we do. If faith truly believes, then it will act on what it believes and prosper accordingly. The greatest things we've ever done in ministry happened because we immediately followed the voice of God in complete obedience. God looks for people who will respond by faith and take action to make His glory known in the earth.

## FAITH RECEIVES

Many times, I've felt the movement of the Spirit upon me and a quickening within my spirit to reach out to receive a particular blessing. But the truth is, faith doesn't wait till later, faith receives now. We've taught people all over the world how to reach into the faith realm to receive. I encourage them to reach up physically with their hands, lift them up above their heads, and to grab hold of the blessings of God by faith. This is practicing how to place the natural into the supernatural dimension. Countless miracles have happened in this way. People receive their healings as they grab hold of them by faith. People have received miracle money and financial blessings as they've reached up to receive them.

Jesus left us an amazing promise. He said, *"Therefore I say to you, whatever things you ask when you pray, believe that you receive them, and you will have them"* (Mark 11:24 NKJV). When God releases revelation, grab hold of it, even if your mind can't understand it, even if you can't seem to grasp it naturally. The natural mind cannot receive or understand the things of the Spirit, but instead, sees them as foolishness. (See 1 Corinthians 2:14.) But you have the mind of Christ and can receive them by the Spirit of God within you. (See 1 Corinthians 2:16.) Spirit receives Spirit.

> WHEN GOD RELEASES REVELATION, GRAB HOLD OF IT, EVEN IF YOUR MIND CAN'T UNDERSTAND IT, EVEN IF YOU CAN'T SEEM TO GRASP IT NATURALLY.

Why not put Mark 11:24 to the test right now? Focus on whatever you need (for yourself, for your home life, your family, or your spiritual and physical wellbeing), and receive it by faith right now. Reach into the faith realm and say, "Faith receives, and so I will receive by faith. I will receive my miracle. Since faith receives, and I have faith, I will receive what I need today." Pull on the heavens. Pull by faith and receive by faith. If you believe, faith will take action, and you will receive.

Sometimes we need faith to trust the revelation that God has given to someone else. Elijah pulled on the heavens for rain because his servant could see a cloud the size of a man's hand. (See 1 Kings 18:43–45.) If we could navigate through these realms together, imagine how far we could reach in the Spirit.

## FAITH REFUSES

I would be remiss if I failed to mention that along with faith having the ability to receive, faith also has the ability and right to refuse. What do I mean by this? Let me illustrate with something that happened to us not long ago. Someone that we didn't know sent us an ungodly piece of artwork in the mail. We never saw it, but we could feel an evil presence on the package. Although the painting had been sent to us, we didn't want it.

Now think about this. While the package had our name and mailing address on the label, we had the right to refuse delivery of it. We told the postal workers to return it to the sender, and they did. Please understand this revelation. In the past, the enemy has lied to you about the things that belonged to you or your family. Sometimes the enemy has put your name and address on sickness, poverty, or oppression and called it a *generational curse*. But just because your name is on it doesn't mean you have to receive it.

Faith has the right to refuse sickness and disease. It has the right to refuse poverty. It has the right to command that anything evil be returned to the sender. You were born to live in the generational blessing of Abraham, Isaac, and Jacob. (See Genesis 24:1; Galatians 3:14.) Don't accept anything less.

## HOW THE FAITH REALM WORKS

How does the faith realm work? To put it in the simplest terms, faith works by love. (See Galatians 5:6.) A few years ago, we received a beautiful Christmas card from one of our ministry partners. It said, "Where there is great love, there are always great miracles." We were touched by those simple words because there was so much wisdom in that short phrase. The Scriptures are clear that if we move in the Spirit—speaking in tongues, prophesying, or doing miracles—but don't have love, we're like a clanging cymbal (see 1 Corinthians 13:1), an annoying sound that doesn't bless anyone. Faith works by love.

If God is love (see 1 John 4:8), then the only way faith can truly work is by God Himself being the driving force behind it. That's why He wants us to become a people who walk in His love. Determine in your spirit to do that, and you will see the result in the function of your faith. Affirm that decision with these words: "No matter what anybody says or does to me, I will walk in love so miracles can be released from my life. I will walk in the Spirit, allowing God to consume every part of me. Everyone else has to deal with their own issues, but I will walk in love, because the only way my faith works is by love. I want to be a conduit for the miraculous. I want to emanate the essence of God's presence. I will walk in love."

Faith works by love, and that's the only way it works. Without love, faith is broken.

## SHIFTING GEARS FROM REALM TO REALM

Faith never leads you into a place of defeat or failure. First John 5:4 tells us that faith always releases the power of God for our victory. So, faith is the beginning point for what God wants to unfold in our lives. It connects us to a fresh anointing that destroys barriers to God's blessing.

In the twenty-third psalm, David eloquently leads us on a beautiful spiritual journey of faith. Faith invited him into the green pastures and led him beside still waters, but it also carried him through the darkest valley because he fully trusted in the Lord as his Shepherd. But notice that it was in this place of pressure, in the presence of his greatest enemy, that the anointing was poured out to overflowing.

We also find ourselves at the end of our own strengths and capabilities before we are fully given to the next realm in the Spirit. But when you are down to nothing, God is always up to something. When you come to the end of yourself, you discover the beautiful beginnings of God. Just as grapes must be crushed to produce new wine and olives must be pressed to produce fresh oil, it is in a place of perfect submission that you will find perfect faith. Then you will pray, like Jesus, *"Not my will, but Yours be done"* (Luke 22:42). Your faith can only take you so far, and then you must surrender yourself to the working of God's Spirit.

> FAITH CAN LEAD YOU THROUGH DIFFICULT TRIALS, BUT THE ANOINTING WILL GIVE YOU THE POWER TO OVERCOME THEM.

Faith can lead you through difficult trials, but the anointing will give you the power to overcome them. Even as God anointed David's head with fresh oil, He desires to anoint us in this day with the oil of His Spirit. This goes beyond the understanding of man as the Spirit invites us into the mind of the miraculous. The anointing is the oil of healing, the oil of provision, the oil of favor, and the oil of joy. Faith activates the realm of the superabundant anointing.

Are you hungry to go deeper in the Spirit? He has greater things prepared for you as you determine to enter into these *Glory Realms*.

When you come to the ends of yourself, you discover the beautiful beginnings of God.

2

# REALMS OF ANOINTING

*The Spirit of the Lord is on me, because he has anointed me to*
*proclaim good news to the poor. He has sent me to proclaim freedom*
*for the prisoners and recovery of sight for the blind, to set the*
*oppressed free, to proclaim the year of the Lord's favor.*
—Luke 4:18–19

The anointing is the manifest power of God that sets us apart. According to the dictionary, the word *anoint* means "to dedicate to the service of God, or to consecrate or make sacred in a ceremony." My friend Chris Harvey defined it as "the favor to go, the grace to do, the power to be, and the strength to continue." I like that definition because it paints a picture of the ability of God to work through us. That's what the anointing is. It is a divine enablement that helps us to accomplish God's supernatural purposes here on earth. The anointing comes from God, but He releases it to men and women so that we might accomplish things through His divine ability, allowing us to do things we cannot do in our own natural strength.

In the Scriptures and throughout Christian tradition, we see oil being used as a symbol of the anointing of God. Oil is thick, fragrant, and contains healing properties. The anointing is the same.

## THE POWER OF ANOINTING

*For the kingdom of God is not a matter of talk but of power.*
(1 Corinthians 4:20)

Although there is a thought process and vocabulary that comes with the anointing of God, this endowment from Him reaches far beyond the intellectual realm. Actually, the only way this power works is if we're willing to let go of our own natural power or control, and cooperate with the power of the Spirit. It is in this place of submission that the raw potential of God is seen clearly as He demonstrates His supernatural ability through our lives. The anointing allows the gifts of the Spirit to function freely.

Proof of this anointing is that when God shows up, things look different. Sometimes the person anointed appears as a different person altogether. The prophet Samuel said, *"The Spirit of the LORD will come powerfully upon you, and you will prophesy with them; and you will be changed into a different person"* (1 Samuel 10:6). Many times, as I first step into the anointing, I can feel this supernatural transition taking place. The inflection of my voice changes, and sometimes my mannerisms do too. This is not something I do on purpose, but, rather, it is evidence of the anointing taking over.

The anointing of God is able to change your personality, behavior, attitudes, and giftedness. I have spoken with many preachers who are actually very shy and would prefer to remain in the background. But when the anointing of God comes upon them, they become as bold as a lion, and you would never imagine their personalities being any different.

As you surrender to the anointing, the impact of that anointing is magnified. When my friend, the late Rev. Edgar Baillie, stepped into the anointing, his right hand changed color. It turned bright red, signaling a surge of healing power flowing through him. This was unusual, but from God.

I knew a woman who had an encounter in the Spirit. Her eye color changed from dark brown to the bluest of blues. Her eyes looked like rivers swirling with God's love.

The anointing will change you too. Don't be afraid of it, but embrace how God desires to show forth His power in and through you.

## THE THREE DIMENSIONS OF THE ANOINTING

*They go from strength to strength, till each appears before God in Zion.*
(Psalm 84:7)

In the same way that there are three realms in the Spirit (and in the last chapter I showed you the three dimensions of faith), you will see that there are also three dimensions when it comes to the anointing. In the Old Testament, we see:

1. The anointing of priests (see Exodus 28:41; 30:30; 40:15; Leviticus 8:12; 21:12; Numbers 3:3; Psalm 133:2)

2. The anointing of prophets (see 1 Kings 19:16; Psalm 105:15; Isaiah 11:2; 1 Corinthians 14:31)

3. The anointing of kings (see 1 Samuel 16:1, 3, 13; 2 Samuel 2:4, 7; 1 Kings 1:34; 1 Chronicles 11:3)

The anointing prepared them to take up their position and (this is key) to do their job. It also activated the mantle over their lives and made them effective in it. In the same way, God releases His anointing on us today so that we can do the job He sets before us. These specific anointings—priestly, prophetic, and kingly—are still available to us.

Spiritually speaking, the anointing is associated with the hand of God, representing the five-fold ministry of apostle, prophet, evangelist, pastor, and teacher. But the anointing isn't just about the five-fold ministry. In its purest flow, the anointing brings a grace to carry out the specific will of God for your life. Without the anointing, your calling could never develop properly, so the Spirit anoints ordinary believers because the task at hand is much greater than the senior leaders of the church can accomplish on their own. The hand of the Spirit anoints men and women to fulfill their high calling as ministers for God wherever they may find themselves.

You are being anointed to do your job. You can be anointed as a student to succeed with your studies. You can be anointed to be a better spouse. You can be anointed as a business person to prosper in every good thing. You can be anointed as a parent to raise your children in the ways of the Lord with the wisdom of heaven. You are anointed to

WITHOUT THE ANOINTING, YOUR CALLING COULD NEVER DEVELOP PROPERLY, SO THE SPIRIT ANOINTS ORDINARY BELIEVERS BECAUSE THE TASK AT HAND IS MUCH GREATER THAN THE SENIOR LEADERS OF THE CHURCH CAN ACCOMPLISH ON THEIR OWN.

do what the Spirit has ordained for you, no matter how impossible that may seem.

If you have a call to the nations, there is an anointing for that too. If you are called to the ministry of helps, there is an anointing for that. For every call, there is a special anointing.

In the anointing, we learn how to grow in grace. John the Baptist grew in grace (see Luke 1:80), and Jesus did too (see Luke 2:40). In this dimension of anointing, we learn how to move in God. It's not about human effort or performance, but about giving ourselves sacrificially to the purposes of the anointing. In the process, we receive grace from the fullness of God's grace. *"Out of his fullness we have all received grace in place of grace already given"* (John 1:16).

There are three distinct expressions of the anointing within the Scriptures:

1. To pour out

2. To smear over

3. To rub in

When the Spirit releases His anointing on us, He's not just giving us a little bit of supernatural empowerment. He's not just putting a drop of it on the top of our heads or in the palms of our hands. He floods us with His anointing.

I want you to see the process of the anointing that God intends to release in our lives in order to empower us for His glory.

## THE OUTPOURING

*Take the anointing oil and anoint him by pouring it on his head.*

(Exodus 29:7)

The definition of the Hebrew word for *"anointing"* includes the biblical expression "to pour out." Joel mentioned this anointing when he prophesied the worldwide arrival of the Holy Spirit:

*I will pour out my Spirit on all people. Your sons and daughters will prophesy, your old men will dream dreams, your young men will see visions. Even on my servants, both men and women, I will pour out my Spirit in those days.* (Joel 2:28–29)

And this is exactly the way the Holy Spirit showed up on the Day of Pentecost. He came in an outpouring of His Spirit. We understand this outpouring of anointing rested *upon* the believers from Luke's account in Acts 2:2–3:

*Suddenly a sound like the blowing of a violent wind came from heaven and filled the whole house where they were sitting. They saw what seemed to be tongues of fire that separated and came to rest on each of them.*

Several years ago, I received a phone call from my friends, Jeremy and Jillene, requesting prayer. For quite some time, they tried to sell their home in Tampa, Florida, but to no avail. They had taken a job out of state, relocated their family, and expected their home to sell quickly, but that didn't prove to be the case. The home had been listed on the real estate market for several months. Nobody seemed interested in even looking at the property, let alone purchasing it. This couple needed a miracle. I prayed with them on the phone and told them I would present these matters to the Spirit during my times of prayer.

I've learned that when we ask God for a miracle, He often responds by giving us divine instructions. When we pray and ask for a breakthrough, we must take time to listen to the instructions He gives us. This is a key for operating in the anointing. God will ask you to do something possible so He can do something impossible.

In the following days, as I prayed about their situation, I kept seeing, in the Spirit, two large bottles of oil. I knew this represented a double portion of anointing. As we have seen, the principal reason God anoints us is to do a job and release breakthrough. Both were needed in this situation.

> WHEN WE PRAY AND ASK FOR A BREAKTHROUGH, WE MUST TAKE TIME TO LISTEN TO THE INSTRUCTIONS HE GIVES US. THIS IS A KEY FOR OPERATING IN THE ANOINTING.

I saw those two bottles being poured out around the property and sensed that this would bring the land into agreement with the anointing. I also saw the oil being poured out around the community as a sign that the anointing would prevail over any opposing spirit that tried to hinder the sale of that home. I told Jeremy and Jillene that oil needed to be poured around their home, and that God would do the miracle.

(I'm not saying that this is what you need to do in order for the same miracle to happen for you. For each situation we pray about, the instructions may be different. Obedience to the voice of the Spirit is the key.)

I knew what we were supposed to do in this situation, but my friends were unable to get back to Florida for quite some time. Interestingly, I was scheduled to be in that part of Florida in a few weeks for ministry. I told them I would go and do what the Spirit required.

When I arrived in Florida weeks later, after my final ministry meeting, I went to a supermarket and purchased the two largest bottles of oil I could find. I laid my hands on them and thanked God for His anointing that would destroy every yoke of bondage. I thanked Him for using this oil as a point of contact for releasing the miracle breakthrough. Even though it was late at night, I drove through the community. As I drove, I poured the oil onto the streets, leaving a trail to signify the blessing that was established. Then I drove to the property and did exactly what I had seen in the Spirit. I walked around its perimeters, pouring out the oil. I anointed every doorpost on the house with oil. A fresh anointing covered the property. A miracle was imminent.

Within days, phone calls poured in to the real estate agent from people requesting to see the property. Then offers poured in, each person trying to outbid the other in order to secure that home. The anointing did its job and brought a supernatural breakthrough of acceleration. The home sold quickly and for more than its listing price.

There are times when the anointing comes upon us and supernatural oil miraculously flows from our hands and feet. This happens to me many times, as well as to others who are in our meetings. I remember this anointing flowing while we ministered in San Diego. Pastor

Mark Griffo attended those meetings and had his hands overflow with oil as he sat in that atmosphere.

Pastor Mark expected this flow would stop after he left the meetings, but it didn't. This impartation continued on and on. Every time He thought about the goodness of God, the oil flowed again—at home, in the church, or out in public—wherever he happened to be. He testified to us weeks later about the opportunities God had given him to minister healing, deliverance, and blessing to others through this miracle sign. We have seen this same impartation happen for many people. It is glorious.

But there are also times when the supernatural oil doesn't flow from our hands. Yet the Spirit assures us that He will anoint whatever we touch. (See Psalm 90:17.) In these times, we release the anointing over cloths, garments, family photos, or store-bought bottles of oil. God uses these anointed objects to accomplish His supernatural purposes. (See Exodus 40:9–11.)

This is what God's anointing will do for you when it is poured into your life. Following the leading of the Holy Spirit is key to releasing the anointing. Then, the anointing that rests *upon* you is able to work supernatural miracles *for* you.

## THE COVERING

*Do not touch my anointed ones; do my prophets no harm.*
(Psalm 105:15)

The second expression of the anointing, mentioned in Scripture, means "to smear over."[1] This gives us an understanding that the Spirit wants to cover us with His anointing.

In biblical times, shepherds smeared anointing oil over their sheep to keep them from being bitten by annoying insects. During the summer months, it was common for nasal flies to attack the heads of the sheep, burrowing deep into their nose and even into their brain. This could cause a severe infection, leading to irritation, disease, or even death, as the sheep would often bash their heads upon rocks and trees in an attempt to find relief from the pain caused by the flies. To protect the sheep, the shepherd made a mixture of olive oil, sulfur, and other spices. He used it to anoint his sheep by smearing it across their foreheads and around their ears and noses. This anointing brought total protection to the sheep.

As David so beautifully sang in his twenty-third psalm, *"You anoint my head with oil; my cup overflows"* (Psalm 23:5). This gives us an understanding that as the Spirit smears His anointing over us, He covers us with a supernatural protection against the attacks of the enemy that try to bring irritation, frustration, sickness, or even death. Being covered by His anointing gives us power over obstacles and the ability to overcome any problem that presents itself.

The anointing oil used to anoint sheep was also fragrant with spices:

> But thanks be to God, who always leads us as captives in Christ's triumphal procession and uses us to spread the aroma of the knowledge of him everywhere. For we are to God the pleasing aroma of Christ among those who are being saved and those who are perishing.
> (2 Corinthians 2:14–15)

As we are anointed, we become the fragrance.

In Old Testament times when the holy incense was burned in the temple in Jerusalem, the fragrance could be smelled all the way to Jericho, a distance of about sixteen miles. Isn't that amazing? The Spirit smears a fragrant anointing over your life that reaches unto heaven, but God is not the only one who smells it. It also reaches out, affecting those around you. Your fragrance is a testimony of God's favor upon your life. This anointing is the power of God that sets us apart.

## THE MARINATING

> You love righteousness and hate wickedness; therefore God, your God, has set you above your companions by anointing you with the oil of joy.
> (Psalm 45:7)

The Hebrew word used here for *"anointing"* is *mashach*, which means "to rub in." When this level of anointing is rubbed into you, your flesh becomes uncomfortable. You might say that it "rubs your flesh the wrong way." Don't panic. You need this to happen because

*(handwritten margin note: Mashach – similar to hebrew word for Messiah)*

where you're going, your flesh can't take you. That flesh must die in order for your spirit to fly.

In the Spirit, these realms build upon each other. When faith and anointing work together, they destroy the yoke of bondage that faith alone cannot break. When this anointing works within us, it deals with our moral character, producing a greater manifestation of the fruit of the Spirit: *"But the fruit of the Spirit is love, joy, peace, forbearance, kindness, goodness, faithfulness, gentleness and self-control. Against such things there is no law"* (Galatians 5:22–23).

The first two dimensions deal with the anointing *upon* us, but this third dimension deals with the anointing *within* us. The reason many ministers can operate in awesome giftings with great supernatural power and still fall morally is because they haven't submitted themselves to this third dimension of the anointing. They haven't allowed it to work its full measure in them.

> WHEN FAITH AND ANOINTING WORK TOGETHER, THEY DESTROY THE YOKE OF BONDAGE THAT FAITH ALONE CANNOT BREAK.

Somebody has said, "The anointing is God's gift to mankind, but integrity is mankind's gift back to God." This is true, but the anointing that allows us to walk in full integrity is only discovered when we submit ourselves completely to the work of God's Spirit. We must become marinated by the anointing, allowing it to be rubbed into every area of our life—spirit, soul, and body.

This anointing demands greater sacrifice. Both Samson and David were anointed by God, but could not support the weight of that anointing. Why? They hadn't allowed it to work throughout every area of their lives.

If we receive the things of the Spirit deeply, an infilling brings tenderness to our soul. This doesn't always happen during the initial outpouring of anointing, but as we spend time in God's presence, the anointing increases. We move from the initial outpouring into the covering, and finally into being marinated with an anointing that supernaturally infiltrates the very core of our being. You can't get to the place in the glory that God wants to take you unless you push through in the anointing that He's given you.

Some people want to skip this process, but you can't afford to do that. You must let the anointing work within you. The anointing comes to do a job, and one of its assignments is marinating you in God's process of preparation.

What God does for us He does in levels—measures, degrees—always moving us step by step. There is a process in the things of the Spirit, but also an acceleration in God that can move you quickly through the process. I've witnessed people being born again one night and beginning their ministry the next day. That is the acceleration of the Spirit. But there is still a spiritual process involved because we need both the anointing *upon* and the anointing *within*.

One of the Scriptures that speaks about this anointing being "rubbed in" is James 5:14: *"Is anyone among you sick? Let them call the elders of the church to pray over them and anoint them with oil in the name of the Lord."*

With an understanding of what that anointing looks like, this passage of Scripture paints a beautiful picture. The people of God surround someone who is sick and bathes them with the oil of the Holy Spirit and the prayer of faith.

> THE ANOINTING COMES TO DO A JOB, AND ONE OF ITS ASSIGNMENTS IS MARINATING YOU IN GOD'S PROCESS OF PREPARATION.

Sometimes we're too quick to move forward. At times, the process of the anointing may require greater sacrifices of time and effort on our part in order to see the fullest effect. Frequently, I listen to worship music and allow myself to soak for great periods of time in the impartation of the anointing.

I recently recorded a powerful healing CD[2] on which I speak the Word of God and make prophetic declarations over those who are sick. Already, many have spent hours listening to that CD. We have received testimonies of God working healing miracles in the lives of those who took the time to saturate themselves under the influence of that healing anointing.

God fully immerses us in His anointing oil, saturates us, and gets us ready to do the job set before us. There is healing in the anointing. There are miracles in the anointing. The anointing *within* us protects the anointing that has been placed *upon* us. The more we are filled with the anointing, the greater the thrust we have as we move forward into the glory realm.

## GIVING THE ANOINTING AWAY

In the early days, when the Spirit began to manifest the golden glory in our lives and ministry, Janet and I lived in San Diego, California. There was such a manifestation of golden glory that our apartment was filled with it. Everything was covered.

One of the first things God told us to do with the golden glory was to gather it up and give it to other people. That, I believe, is what kept the manifestation active. If we keep the things of God to ourselves, they diminish and even dissipate. Give away what God has blessed you with so it can be a blessing to others. In this way, you position yourself to enter into a continual flow.

When we asked the Lord what all of this meant, He spoke to us from Acts 19:11–12: *"God did extraordinary miracles through Paul, so that even handkerchiefs and aprons that had touched him were taken to the sick, and their illnesses were cured and the evil spirits left them."*

Many people like to call these "prayer cloths," but I don't see prayer anywhere in that Scripture. What the Scripture tells me is that God did an extraordinary thing through Paul. A flow of supernatural anointing was released from his life onto those cloths. People brought their handkerchiefs and aprons, and these were used for working miracles. When those anointed cloths were taken to people's homes, their loved ones got healed, delivered, and set free.

Why did all of this happen? The anointed cloths were a point of contact for power to be released with miracles and breakthroughs. We realized that we needed to gather the golden glory, place it on the cloths, and give it to others, since it was a manifestation of God's power. We knew that as we distributed these anointed cloths, people would receive healing, salvation, and deliverance.

We shared this with the people in our church. They took the anointed cloths and put them under the pillows of the unsaved and gave them to the sick. We saw wonderful results. Testimonies of healings and the salvation of family members were reported.

We sent out a few emails to other friends, telling them what we were doing. Soon we were flooded with of thousands of emails from people everywhere, asking for one of those anointed cloths. We never considered what all of this would cost in postage, but when God gives you a vision, He always brings the provision. And He was faithful again. God's glory is our hope, and pursuing His call on our lives is top priority. By God's grace, we were able to mail thousands of anointed cloths all over the world. Testimonies poured in.

Caroline, from North Devon, England, wrote,

> Thank you for sending the cloth so soon. I work in a Christian holiday center, and recently a lady came in with crutches. She had broken her ankle and she was in agony. When I saw her that morning, she was in bad shape. She couldn't sleep because the pain was too much. I offered to pray for her and I placed the cloth on her ankle. God is good. She is now walking without pain and without crutches. The best part is that she is a doctor. I used this cloth to bless others as well and I also saw instant healing.

One man in South Africa received an anointed cloth. The Spirit soon revealed to him things in his life that he needed to deal with, specifically unforgiveness and bitterness that he held against other people. "You need to forgive those people," the Spirit told him. "You need to let go of those roots of bitterness." As he forgave each of the people who had wronged him, ten different diseases lifted off of his body, making him completely whole.

All these years later, we continue sending anointed cloths out to people who write and ask for them. Sometimes they are covered with golden glory. At other times, we've anointed them with supernatural oil. People place these cloths in their clothing, wallets, or specific places in their homes, depending upon their area of need, and God works the miracle because His anointing brings breakthrough.

## THE TRANSITION FROM ANOINTING TO GLORY

We use the realms of faith and the realm of the anointing to bring us into the realms of glory. The anointing enables us to swim in the river of God. Prophetically speaking, when that river flows, we are enabled to do supernatural works. We swim in that river, doing the best we can, empowered by the Holy Spirit's anointing. Then comes a seeming contradiction. When the glory arrives, it actually *disables* us. So, why would God enable then disable us? The anointing enables us, and we swim in the river of God. The glory disables us, because when it comes, we surf on the waves of the Spirit's flow.

There is an ease that comes by surfing that's much different from the intense physical labor that is required when you're swimming. God's Word declares, *"Let us labor therefore to enter into that rest"* (Hebrews 4:11 KJV). There is a laboring, a time of working to get into the rest, but then, when you are finally in the rest, everything comes with great ease. It's not that you are no longer willing to do more. It's that the Spirit is now carrying you along, and you experience an ease. You flow in the glory, whereas you had to press into the anointing. You go from a place of being empowered to carry yourself, to a place of being carried in ease by the Spirit.

Are you hungry to go deeper in the Spirit? He has greater things prepared for you as you determine to enter into these *Glory Realms*.

3

# REALMS OF GLORY

*Now the Lord is the Spirit, and where the Spirit of the Lord is,
there is freedom. And we all, who with unveiled faces contemplate
the Lord's glory, are being transformed into his image with ever-
increasing glory, which comes from the Lord, who is the Spirit.*
—2 Corinthians 3:17–18

**S**ome things in the Spirit cannot be grasped by faith alone. There are also some things in the Spirit that cannot be released through an anointing. That's why we must learn how to bring forth the glory. Faith says God is present, the anointing says God rewards, but the glory says, "I Am."

In a moment's time, the glory can capture your miracle and overshadow the most difficult situations. The glory is not limited by time, space, or circumstance. Neither is it limited by the mind of man or earthly ability. It is eternal and flows into those dimensions with every good and perfect gift that comes from above. There are no limitations in the glory realm.

What is the glory? God is the glory, and the glory is God. The glory is God's fullness. It's His manifest presence, His character, His nature, His ability, His provision, and the weight and splendor of His majesty. It is the essence of His beauty. The glory is all that He is and all that He has. Everything about God is glorious, and He wants us to know Him in the fullness of His glory because He is the God of Glory. (See Psalm 138:5; Acts 7:2.)

Isaiah 6:1 says, *"In the year that King Uzziah died, I saw the Lord, high and exalted, seated on a throne; and the train of his robe filled the temple."*

What happens when God shows up in the temple, in the place of His dwelling? What happens when He shows up anywhere? His manifest presence, His glory, fills the temple, and as a result, sickness and poverty can no longer stay in that temple. When God fills the temple with His glory, everything that is not glorious must go to make room for the glory. This is why we need the glory now more than ever before.

Determine to open up more and more to the glory. In the glory, there is increase, there is abundance, there is healing, there is life, there is wholeness, there is provision, there is prosperity, and there is deliverance.

Isaiah continued:

> *Above him were seraphim, each with six wings: With two wings they covered their faces, with two they covered their feet, and with two they were flying. And they were calling to one another: "Holy, holy, holy is the LORD Almighty; the whole earth is full of his glory." At the sound of their voices the doorposts and thresholds shook and the temple was filled with smoke.* (Isaiah 6:2–4)

That was the glory cloud. When the glory cloud appears, discord and disunity, problems and difficulties have to go.

We know that the temple God is interested in today is not one made with bricks and mortar. *We* are now the temple of the Holy Spirit, and the smoke of His presence must manifest in our daily lives. Welcome it, expect it, and rejoice in it when it comes.

## INVITE THE GLORY CLOUD

Invite God to fill your temple with the smoke of His presence. It is a cloud of abundance. Release it to your family and friends. Release it to your coworkers and associates. Let that cloud surround your life so that you carry a new dimension of goodness and grace with you wherever you go.

Daniel had a similar vision of God's glory. He said:

> *As I looked, thrones were set in place, and the Ancient of Days took his seat. His clothing was as white as snow; the hair of his head was white like wool. His throne was flaming with fire, and its wheels were*

*all ablaze. A river of fire was flowing, coming out from before him. Thousands upon thousands attended him; ten thousand times ten thousand stood before him. The court was seated, and the books were opened.*                                          (Daniel 7:9–10)

John saw it too. He said:

*On the Lord's Day I was in the Spirit, and I heard behind me a loud voice like a trumpet, which said: "Write on a scroll what you see and send it to the seven churches…" I turned around to see the voice that was speaking to me. And when I turned I saw seven golden lampstands, and among the lampstands was someone like a son of man, dressed in a robe reaching down to his feet and with a golden sash around his chest. The hair on his head was white like wool, as white as snow, and his eyes were like blazing fire. His feet were like bronze glowing in a furnace, and his voice was like the sound of rushing waters. In his right hand he held seven stars, and coming out of his mouth was a sharp, double-edged sword. His face was like the sun shining in all its brilliance. When I saw him, I fell at his feet as though dead.*                                          (Revelation 1:10–17)

The voice John heard called him higher. The Spirit calls to us today to come up, to ascend into the very presence of the Lord. He wants to show us wonderful things. He wants to reveal His glory to us and through us.

## THE SPIRIT'S INVITATION

We have the Spirit's invitation, and there are no limits, no boundaries. Distance is no longer a factor. Age is no longer a factor. Past performance is no longer a factor. He calls all of us higher. Get out of your own mind and into the mind of the Spirit. Come up higher where the sea is as clear as crystal, and heavenly sounds crash like thunder. Hear the voice like many waters coming from the Great I Am. Hear the angels, the elders, and the creatures singing, "Worthy! Worthy! Worthy is the Lamb! Blessing and honor and glory and power unto Him!" (See Revelation 5:12–13.) Open your spiritual eyes, for the veil has been torn.

There are now no limits. Open your spiritual ears to hear. Open your spirit to receive revelation. Open your heart to receive. Stand at God's throne. Deep is crying unto deep. Let Him take you deeper. Let the cloud of His glory gather about you as you join the angels in crying out, "Holy is the Lord!"

Clouds bring rain. Let that rain saturate your spirit. Rain births a harvest, so get ready to reap. Go ahead, thrust your sickle into the great harvest from this cloud. Stand in agreement with the saints of all ages, with the angelic beings, and with the elders on high. Lend your voice to the sound of praise for the Creator of all things. Eternity bows at His name. He will reign forever! Set your thoughts on the glory realm and live by the truth of God's Word. Gaze upon its unsearchable beauty.

Who could ever measure His Word? As we are obedient to it, we shall reign with Him, for He is coming in clouds of glory! Feel the swirling wind of His presence. Bask in the atmosphere of heaven. You are in Him, and He is in you. Stand in His glory. He fills the temple. Feel the flood of grace, mercy, and compassion coming to you even now through the cloud. Lay hold of the divine wisdom and illumination that come to you now in the cloud of God's glory.

As your spirit rises, allow the constraints of the flesh to fall away. Be set free from any remaining shackles. Know that in this glory realm there are no impossibilities. In this realm, nothing is too difficult for God.

KNOW THAT IN THIS GLORY REALM THERE ARE NO IMPOSSIBILITIES. IN THIS REALM, NOTHING IS TOO DIFFICULT FOR GOD.

As you begin to navigate within the glory realm, you will hear things you have never heard before and see things you have never seen before. At times, this will offend your natural mind because it is so new to you. The Spirit desires for us to operate on a higher level. He also desires to give you something, impart something to you, open something to you. Your part is to open yourself as never before. Be willing to step fully into this cloud that you have never experienced before. *Let the glory come!*

## THE IDENTITY OF THE GLORY

Whereas the anointing defines the power of God, the glory defines the person of God. When we consider the trifold nature of God's identity, revealed through the Father, Son, and Holy Spirit, we behold the greater revelation of this glory. Some aspects of God's identity can only be fully realized in the glory dimension.

The apostle Paul identified God as *"the Father of glory."* *"That the God of our Lord Jesus Christ, the Father of glory, may give unto you the spirit of wisdom and revelation in the knowledge of him"* (Ephesians 1:17 KJV).

Ask God to reveal Himself to you as the Father of glory. Let Him reveal Himself as the Source of all glory. Everything about Him is glorious. When you view Him this way, your spirit eyes will be filled with glory.

Many Scriptures speak of Jesus and the glory of God. Through the person of Jesus Christ, the Son of God, we see the unfolding of God's glory in an even greater way. The psalmist David sang about Him as *"the King of glory"*: *"Lift up your heads, you gates; lift them up, you ancient doors, that the King of glory may come in"* (Psalm 24:7).

God wants you to know Him as the King of glory in your life. As you open up more and more, you create an entrance for the royal procession of heaven to move in and make way for kingly blessings. As you begin to know the glory in this way, get ready to receive both the spiritual and physical manifestation of abundance.

John the beloved recognized: *"The Word became flesh and made his dwelling among us. We have seen his glory, the glory of the one and only Son, who came from the Father, full of grace and truth"* (John 1:14). He also recognized the miracle ministry of Jesus that produced glorious outcomes. (See John 2:11.) James called Jesus *"the Lord of glory"* (James 2:1 KJV), and the apostle Paul proclaimed that Jesus Christ inside of us is *"the hope of glory"* (Colossians 1:27). Right now, ask God to give you a revelation of Jesus in His glory. In the past, you may have had a revelation of His saving power or His healing touch, but now He wants to give you a revelation of the radiance of His glory.

It's His glorious light that brings illumination. (See Revelation 21:23–26.) *"The Son is the radiance of God's glory and the exact representation of his being, sustaining all things by his powerful word"* (Hebrews 1:3).

You will discover that the deeper you go into the glory, the deeper the glory will go into you. The more you give yourself to this realm, the more you will find yourself thinking of the glory, speaking about the glory, and moving in the glory. When you begin to move in this glory, others may not be able to understand what is happening in your life, especially if they haven't yet received the revelation of it. For those who have never experienced the glory, these things seem foolish (see 1 Corinthians 2:14), for they are only discerned by the Spirit. Never become discouraged by other people's lack of spiritual growth or misunderstanding of what is happening in your life. Stay focused on the glory, and let it grow in you. The radiance of glory upon you will speak for itself.

When in public after spending hours in the manifest presence of God, we are often covered in the golden glory, but the responses we receive from others can be either positive or negative. When people we meet sense the glory on our lives and respond favorably, we realize that these are the individuals God has sent us to minister to.

Although others see the same manifestation, they may not be moved to any response or may respond negatively. In the early days of our ministry, when this happened, we became grieved, wondering why some people couldn't sense the same glory we were experiencing. We were just beginning to learn how to discern and flow in cooperation with this glory. At times, we've received persecution from people in the church because of the manifestations that take place in our lives, but these things no longer bother us. In speaking of spiritual persecution, the apostle Peter introduced the Holy Spirit as *"the Spirit of glory."*  *"If you are insulted because of the name of Christ, you are blessed, for the Spirit of glory and of God rests on you"* (1 Peter 4:14). *Let the glory come!*

## SHINE IN THE GLORY

*Arise, shine, for your light has come, and the glory of the LORD rises upon you. See, darkness covers the earth and thick darkness is over the peoples, but the LORD rises upon you and his glory appears over you. Nations will come to your light, and kings to the brightness of your dawn.*                                            (Isaiah 60:1–3)

The Holy Spirit is the Spirit of glory, and His glory is realized even greater in the midst of darkness. It causes us to arise and shine. Even as the world grows darker with threats of nuclear war, famine, new diseases, and all sorts of wickedness, our spiritual light will shine brighter in the darkness. The glory releases heaven's radiance upon our countenance and causes our spirits to shine. That makes a total difference in your life. When we get into the glory, the atmosphere is filled with the visible *shekinah*. At times in our corporate meetings, we'll see a golden substance fall through the air. Sometimes it falls like rain, and at others it swirls like a whirlwind in the atmosphere. There is a brilliance in the glory, and God wants to release that brilliance over you.

Several years ago during a ministry trip, we traveled with a team in two vehicles through the state of Pennsylvania. As we praised and worshiped the Lord, the weight of God's glory increased inside the vehicles. At one point, golden glory rained down inside our vans. Our praise grew stronger, and the glory increased and became thicker.

Suddenly, the manifestation of this golden glory changed to an emerald green substance. I knew that the Spirit was speaking to us regarding financial miracles. We pulled over at the next exit, parked our vehicles at the side of the road, and jumped out of the vans, praising the Lord wildly with this manifestation of glory sparkling all around us.

We had stopped in front of a home. A women who lived there saw us dancing and was intrigued by the spectacle. She came outside, saw the glory upon us, and asked what we were doing. In reply, I asked her if she had ever seen a miracle before. She told me that she went to church, but could not recall ever seeing a miracle. We shared our experience. I told her that the emerald-colored manifestation represented financial miracles and asked if she needed one. Tears streamed down her face as she shared how earlier that day, she had lost her job.

Standing in front of that woman's home, we joined in prayer, thanking God for his miracle sign and for the financial miracle being released into her life. We gave her our contact information, got back in the vehicles, and continued our journey home. Several weeks later that woman contacted our office and shared her testimony. Our visit had deeply encouraged her and resulted in a financial miracle—an even better paying job. Divine appointments happen in the glory.

The Bible speaks of a shining that comes in the presence of God. It happened to Moses when he had gone up the mountain to spend time with the Lord. When he came back down, his face shone so radiantly that it had to be covered. His face radiated light as if illuminated by a powerful light source. For a time, Moses had to keep a veil over his face because the glory blinded the people who looked upon him.

While ministering in Budapest, Hungary, a woman who was in those meetings had an awesome encounter with the glory of God. Her feet literally lit up like light bulbs. This radiance glowed through the sneakers she wore (see Psalm 119:105; Isaiah 52:7; Revelation 1:15) and shone on other objects that surrounded her. This manifestation of the glory caused that woman to dedicate her life fully to the purposes of God. We have a photo of it and love showing it to people for encouragement. She will never be the same. And you will never be the same when you're impacted by the goodness of God. God's glory in and on our lives makes a difference!

That's the kind of glory with which God wants to fill you, causing you to shine. It will increase your witness and influence to the point that no one can deny the power of God in you. When they look at you, all they can see is God. Just as Isaiah foretold, the glory of God's presence draws others to the brightness of your dawn. *Let the glory come!*

## THE THREE DIMENSIONS OF GLORY

God's glory includes three different dimensions. Each one works with the others to reveal the whole.

### THE DOXA *GLORY*

*When the Son of Man comes in his glory, and all the angels with him, he will sit on his glorious throne.* (Matthew 25:31)

This verse describes the first dimension known as the *doxa* glory. The word *doxa* comes from the Greek and means "honor, renown, and splendor." It speaks of an exalted state or a most glorious condition of being. Doxa glory represents the perfect state of blessedness promised to believers and connects us with the excellency and kingly majesty of Jesus Christ. Within the Scriptures, we find it used in 2 Corinthians 3:18, where it gives us the understanding that we move in the Spirit from glory to glory, or from doxa to doxa. We go from one level of splendor to the next as we continue to move in God.

We must never think that we've seen all there is to see in God. So much more exists for those who choose to live in this glory realm. In it, we go from one exalted state to the next.

Although the manifestation of glory in this dimension is intangible, the indication that you're experiencing the doxa glory, is that you are suddenly aware of Jesus's kingly position. In this dimension, you surrender to His rightful authority as ruler over all.

Several years ago, I had the opportunity to spend some time with Dr. Terry Law, who in the past, powerfully impacted the nation of China. (Recently, the thrust of his ministry has shifted to the Middle East.) He shared testimonies with me about countless people having visions, dreams, and encounters with Jesus as the King of Kings and the one true Savior of humanity. Jesus is appearing and making Himself known even to those who have never heard the gospel before. This is the doxa glory, and it is opening up the way for a flood of souls to come into the kingdom of God.

WE MUST NEVER THINK THAT WE'VE SEEN ALL THERE IS TO SEE IN GOD. SO MUCH MORE EXISTS FOR THOSE WHO CHOOSE TO LIVE IN THIS GLORY REALM.

Many years ago, while ministering in Natchez, Mississippi, we had a powerful encounter with God's doxa glory. During the morning session, I was leading worship, when suddenly the atmosphere shifted, and the presence of God's holiness filled the sanctuary. We were aware, like Moses at the burning bush (see Exodus 3:5), that we were standing on holy ground. Many people came forward to the altar area and lay prostrate before the Lord. The fear of the Lord with intense reverence and honor became our posture.

Then it happened. All of us felt the Lord Jesus Himself walk into the room. There was such peace, such power, such love, and such presence! I never saw Him in this encounter, for, as much as I wanted to, I could not open my eyes in that moment. But the awareness of Jesus in the room was undeniable. He was there. He was healing. He was ministering. He was touching His people.

The encounter lasted for hours, although it didn't seem that way in the natural. We never broke for lunch, but remained in that holy stillness all afternoon. When people arrived for the evening meeting, we were still at the altar in awe of the glory we had experienced. That encounter was life-changing for me. Through it, I received an impartation of healing from the Healer Himself.

It was the doxa glory. It may come to you through a dream, an impression, a vision or trance, or in the midst of your worship, but when this dimension of glory is present, you are fully aware that Jesus is Lord.

## *THE* SHEKINAH *GLORY*

*You came to greet him with rich blessings and placed a crown of pure gold on his head.*
(Psalm 21:3)

The second dimension is the visible glory of God, the *shekinah* glory. This means "dwelling" or "settling" and, in a fuller meaning, is described as the transformational glory in which visible change occurs in the atmosphere. The appearance of the cloud by day and the fire by night in Moses's time was the appearance of the shekinah glory. (See Exodus 40:34–38.) The shekinah glory is also seen in the imagery of the thrones and robes in Isaiah 6:1 and Jeremiah 17:12. Ezekiel encountered the shekinah glory, and said, *"And there before me was the glory of the God of Israel, as in the vision I had seen in the plain"* (Ezekiel 8:4).

*Glory* is one of the most common words found in the Scriptures, and the word *shekinah*, found within rabbinical literature, is several times in *The Amplified Version*. (See Exodus 40:34; Leviticus 9:23;

Ezekiel 9:3, 10:3, 19, 11:22; Romans 9:4.) We find an understanding of the appearance of this shekinah glory when we read Jesus's words in Matthew 18:20: *"For where two or three gather in my name, there am I with them."* That is His shekinah presence.

As I noted earlier, the Spirit wants to reveal His shekinah glory to us, and we should always expect to encounter it when in corporate gatherings of believers. When I minister in the glory, I ask people to check their hands to see if the shekinah is manifesting as tiny sparkles coming up through the pores of the skin or falling upon them in the atmosphere of divine presence. Frequently, people see the glory in this way, and it is wonderful.

Seeing the shekinah glory upon a person is never a sign of holiness or that this person is more anointed than another. When this glory comes, it appears on the young and the old, the saved and the unsaved. It is a sign of the glory, not of man, a sign that God desires to release His glory upon the nations. (See Genesis 18:18; Exodus 9:16; Joshua 4:24; 1 Kings 8:60; Psalm 96:3.)

Many times we use this visible shekinah glory as a way to witness to those who are in need of salvation. And it works. *Let the glory come!*

## THE KABOD *GLORY*

*The priests could not enter the temple of the LORD because the glory of the LORD filled it.*　　　　　　　　　(2 Chronicles 7:2)

The third dimension of visible glory is *kabod. Kabod* is a Hebrew word that means "heaviness" or "weight." The kabod glory is the realm of glory in which we encounter the weightiness of God. This is the cloud of glory. Often we will feel the glory as it descends into our midst. When this happens, I encourage the people to lift their hands into the kabod realm and sense the blessing and goodness of God. It is the manifestation of His greatness and superiority.

Sometimes this weighty glory presents in the midst of trials and brief afflictions. (See 2 Corinthians 4:17.) This is God turning our situations around and reminding us of His promises. Instead of feeling the weight of the world, we feel the weight of the glory of God.

From within this cloud, we hear the voice of God speak with revelatory clarity. The Lord spoke to Moses, *"I am going to come to you in a dense cloud, so that the people will hear me speaking with you"* (Exodus 19:9). I have personally found that within this realm of glory, fresh insight and revelatory understanding come with ease. When I enter this dimension of God, I make sure to have a pen and pad of paper close by. As He speaks, I take notes.

Many times, in corporate worship, I find myself enveloped within this cloud and in that realm of glory, receive downloads for that particular meeting. Sometimes the Lord gives me names of people to pray for, or healing action that needs taken, or He places a song in my spirit to sing. This cloud is filled with everything we need.

In Psalm 91:1 (KJV), David sang about *"the secret place of the Most High."* In verse 1, this beautiful psalm also speaks about the cloud canopy or *"Shadow of the Almighty."* This is the cloud of God's glory, and within that cloud, we find refuge and deliverance (see verses 2–3), protection and healing (see verses 4–10), and angelic interaction (see verses 11–12).

Scripture tells us that Jesus is coming back in the cloud. (See Luke 21:27.) We must learn to stand together within the smoke of His presence, inviting the corporate cloud. Eventually, our praise will spark His return. Let us invite this realm of God into our midst. *Let the glory come!*

## OPEN DOORS IN THE GLORY

*Your gates will always stand open, they will never be shut, day or night, so that people may bring you the wealth of the nations—their kings led in triumphal procession.* (Isaiah 60:11)

The glory opens doors that cannot be shut. It is, even now, opening doors for you. As the Scriptures declare, *"The LORD makes firm the steps of the one who delights in him"* (Psalm 37:23). When you walk in the glory, you have nothing to fear. You no longer have to worry about doors being opened for you. Your gates will always stand open.

Jesus said, *"I am the door. If anyone enters by me, he will be saved and will go in and out and find pasture"* (John 10:9 ESV). Not only will your gates stand open, but also, He is the Door. Any time you enter in the glory, there's an open door, because *He* is your open Door. You don't need any other open door but Him. You need God doors; you need glory doors to be opened to you—and He *is* the Door.

> WHEN YOU WALK IN THE GLORY, YOU HAVE NOTHING TO FEAR. YOU NO LONGER HAVE TO WORRY ABOUT DOORS BEING OPENED FOR YOU. YOUR GATES WILL ALWAYS STAND OPEN.

If you are facing sickness today, Jesus is the Door to health. Just step through. If you are facing poverty today, Jesus is the Door to wealth. Just step through. Prosperity lies on the other side. If you need a miracle today, Jesus is the Door to the miraculous. Just step through and walk into the miracle realm. The door is open.

Many people are praying, "Oh, God, please give me an open door." Well, you've got it. You have the best open Door you could ever hope for. Step right into Him. When you step into the glory, you get everything you need. When you step into the glory, you're stepping into the fullness of God. And, as we move in glory realms, the open Door is before us.

If a door is shut, don't become discouraged. Jesus is an open Door. People get upset when certain doors seem to close on them, but the Scriptures show us that God will open doors that no man can shut. (See Revelation 3:8.) So if a door seems shut to you, don't worry about it; God is still the open Door. Look for the openings He has made for you. The Lord has greater opportunities awaiting you.

You may have thought your blessing would come a certain way, but the Spirit is saying, "No, it's over here in the glory realm. Lift your vision a little bit higher to see that I am the open Door. I will provide for your every need."

I have seen well-meaning people become quickly and easily sidetracked by following their problems. If you focus on your lack, you will always feel insufficient. When we focus on the glory, we begin to place our trust in the answer. *Let the glory come!*

## THE SPONTANEITY OF THE GLORY

Following the leading of God's glory often causes us to move into unusual places in unusual ways and teaches us to be spontaneous. Sister Jane Lowder, director of Calvary Campground in Ashland, Virginia, told me early in my ministry, "Brother Joshua, you must always be ready to sing, to prophesy, to receive an offering, or to deliver a message. Be ready in season and out of season." I've never forgotten her words. They have carried me a great distance in the Spirit, and I'm grateful for that advice. We must prepare ourselves to carry the glory. We must prepare ourselves to deliver and release it in the places where the Spirit sends us.

Most of all, we must commit to moving in the Spirit as He directs. When I minister from the pulpit, I always have a message prepared, but am more committed to the glory than to my message. If God uses my message, I'm grateful. If God wants to use my song, I'm willing to sing it. But more than anything else, I want to flow with Him where He leads.

We must learn the spontaneity of the glory that carries us on the ebb and flow of the Spirit. If your teaching doesn't bring the glory, maybe your song will. If your song doesn't bring the glory, maybe your giving will. In any situation, find what brings forth the most glory, and do more of it.

At times while ministering, I became aware that my giving would bring a release. I instructed my workers to distribute every book and CD that was on my resource table to those present in the meeting. We've sown thousands of resources in this way, sometimes distributing thousands at one time. The glory rested upon our giving and brought forth a new revelation of God.

After one such service, a woman testified that this action spoke louder than any message could. Through it, she was released from the fear of lack and taken into a new joy of giving because of the atmosphere created in that room. *Let the glory come!*

## HOW THE GLORY REALM OPERATES

The anointing empowers us to fulfill the Great Commission. "*He* [Jesus] *said to them, 'Go into all the world and preach the gospel to all creation'"* (Mark 16:15). The Spirit gives us His anointing, pours it out, smears it all over us, and rubs it into us. Then He asks, "What will you do with this?" And we must answer, "I will go out and seek those who are lost and need to be saved, those who are sick and need to be healed, and those who are bound and need to be delivered." When we get out there and begin to do the work, something shifts. Blessing comes in obedience.

We see this happening in the first church in Acts. In the upper room encounter, they were empowered by the anointing of the Holy Spirit to speak the Word of God with boldness and for one-on-one miracle ministry. The results were amazing. Thousands came to believe.

As we read farther, we see scenarios where the vastness of the crowd required more than a one-on-one ministry, and the glory moved in. The apostles called on the Lord: *"Stretch out your hand to heal and perform signs and wonders through the name of your holy servant Jesus"* (Acts 4:30). With this, a deluge of miracles was released upon the masses.

We do our part in the anointing, then God does His part in the glory! Pastor Guillermo Maldonado says it like this, "Faith calls the anointing, but the anointing calls the glory."[1]

Can you see how these three realms come together and form a new dimension? The power shifts from *dunamis*, which is the anointing (miraculous power, might, and strength), into *episkiazo*, which is the New Testament cloud of glory, an overshadowing, supernatural influence.

Peter walked in this new dimension of God to such a degree that:

*People brought the sick into the streets and laid them on beds and mats so that at least Peter's shadow might fall on some of them as he passed by. Crowds gathered also from the towns around Jerusalem, bringing their sick and those tormented by impure spirits, and all of them were healed.* (Acts 5:15–16)

This shows how the shift from anointing into glory is a shift from working personal miracles to moving into a pervading influence with the atmosphere of heaven.

As we work in the anointing, God works in the glory. We hear and obey the simple instruction of God, and get ready to move into a greater realm. When the glory comes, we stand in the glory and allow God to do His work.

> WHEN THE GLORY COMES, WE STAND IN THE GLORY AND ALLOW GOD TO DO HIS WORK.

The glory is the highest level of power known to man. In the Scriptures, we read about this *episkiazo* that over-shadowed Peter, James, and John on the mountaintop where they witnessed the physical Transfiguration of Christ, and the appearance of Elijah and Moses. (See Matthew 17:5; Mark 9:7; Luke 9:35.) This same glory over-shadowed the Virgin Mary and implanted a miracle within her womb. (See Luke 1:35.) In the realms of glory, I have seen those who suffered with infertility find their miracle. Healing through the anointing is no longer required in the atmosphere of glory because, in that atmosphere, sickness can no longer exist.

You don't need the touch of man, but a direct impartation from heaven. All that is required is yielding to the glory realm. In this realm, past, present, and future are all right now. There is no time because the glory is the realm of eternity.

Preaching and prophesying are no longer required in the atmosphere of glory. God gave us these tools in the anointing to establish the glory realm. Once it comes, we yield to the revelation of heaven. His instruction is enough.

As previously noted, when the cloud fell upon the priests at the dedication of Solomon's Temple, they could no longer do what they normally did because of the weight of the glory. (See 2 Chronicles 5:14.) In this dimension, your body is supernaturally refreshed because you are ushered into the realm of ease. *Let the glory come!*

## ASKING FOR NATIONS IN THE GLORY

*Ask me, and I will make the nations your inheritance, the ends of the earth your possession.*

(Psalm 2:8)

Years ago, we laid our hands on the map and prayed for two specific nations, Hawaii[2] and Japan, at the same time because we felt a supernatural connection between the two. One evening, after finishing ministry in Atlanta, Georgia, and still lingering in the atmosphere of glory, I felt the Spirit give me a green light about Hawaii. It might seem silly, because who wouldn't want to go to Hawaii? I sensed in my spirit God directing us to go, although we had no contacts or connections there.

In addition, He gave me a specific time frame. Utilizing the realm of faith, I booked airline tickets and hotel for myself, my wife, Janet, and our son, Lincoln. Within a week, we had received an invitation to minister at the Korean Presbyterian Church in Honolulu. The dates they wanted us fell during the time we had already scheduled to be there. More meetings were soon booked, all by divine connections. Our schedule for Hawaii filled before we left.

When we arrived on Oahu, a Presbyterian pastor from Seoul, South Korea, was also visiting. The lady who organized the meetings for us in Hawaii was one of his spiritual daughters. She asked us to meet with and pray for him, as he had been facing some difficult battles. She believed that the ministry of glory would be beneficial for him. Not knowing anything about this minister in the natural, we prayed and felt an anointing for us to minister to him.

Within the first ten minutes of our meeting, the glory of God fell in the room. The pastor was covered in the shekinah glory of God. He sensed God's blessing resting upon him. Through a translator, he excitedly told us about a vision he had for the nation of Japan. Although Korean, he was organizing the largest Christian gathering in the history of Japan and wanted us to be a part of it. The glory opens supernatural doors of opportunity for you. There are realms within the realm.

The minister's name was Yong Jo Ha. He was the leader of Onnuri Community Church, the second largest congregation in South Korea with more than fifty thousand members. His spiritual daughter later told us, "It's an absolute miracle that he invited you to come to Japan and minister with him only ten minutes after meeting him. He has never done such a thing. The glory made the difference." If we want to see God's purposes accelerated in the earth, we must become people of the glory.

Two months later, I stood on the platform in the world's third largest indoor arena, the Saitama Super Arena in Tokyo, Japan, ministering to a crowd of nearly thirty-five thousand people. Within minutes of my taking the stage, the glory of God manifested. Countless people received miracles in that glory realm. Steve Yoo, a well-known Asian pop star, performed at the event. During that move of the glory, his wife, Christine Oh, received a miraculous gold filling in her tooth. They were elated, filled with the joy of the Lord. Several actors from the Korean soap opera *Winter Sonata* also attended and received the manifestation of golden glory upon their hands, clothes, and faces. It was life-changing for them.

Later that evening when the altar call was made, eleven thousand people came forward to give their lives to Christ. It was the largest response in the history of Japan. God gave us the nation because we had asked for it in the glory. Since then, we have ministered all over Japan. The glory multiplies your impact and increases your witness. We must learn how to live in these realms, how to operate in these realms, and how to birth God's purposes in the glory.

> **IF WE WANT TO SEE GOD'S PURPOSES ACCELERATED IN THE EARTH, WE MUST BECOME PEOPLE OF THE GLORY.**

We've felt the urgency to ask God for nations, but you may feel the urgency to ask Him for your family. Lay your hands on photos of your loved ones, call out their names, sing over them, prophesy over them, and watch the glory rise upon them. Allow God to stir in you a passion for those who are lost. Allow Him to birth a heavenly vision of transformation within your spirit. See God move in His glory, then proclaim it with your lips. *Let the glory come!*

## BIRTHING GOD'S PURPOSES IN THE GLORY

*Who has ever heard of such things? Who has ever seen things like this? Can a country be born in a day or a nation be brought forth in a moment? Yet no sooner is Zion in labor than she gives birth to her children.* (Isaiah 66:8)

The anointing is a personal touch which can be transmitted from person to person, whereas the glory is a corporate or atmospheric impartation that comes to accelerate the purposes of God in the earth. In order to make a spiritual impact on a territorial, regional, or national level, it is imperative that you learn how to birth things in the glory. The question has been asked, "Can a nation be saved in a day?" And the answer is unreservedly, "YES!" In the glory, it is possible.

Earlier, I shared the testimony of Kangiqsujuaq, Nunavik, a village in the Canadian Arctic. They experienced the touch of glory to such a degree that every resident was saved and filled with the Spirit. We were blessed to introduce the last three unsaved people to the life-shifting salvation of Christ.

The glory drew the first one, a Kativik regional police officer, to the altar of the Full Gospel Church, where I was ministering. He went back and told two prisoners in the jail house what had just happened to him. They were so fascinated that the police officer called and asked us to come to the jail and explain everything to them. When we arrived at the jail, the prisoners' families were already there. An air of excitement about the things of the Spirit filled the room. We grabbed the prisoners' hands through their cell doors and led them in the sinner's prayer. They felt the same touch of glory that the rest of the community was experiencing.

I love the fact that the glory is not reserved for a select few, but is available for anyone who wants it. Those willing to receive it and flow in it will be carried the farthest in this next move of the Spirit. It won't matter what social status, economic condition, or educational degree you have. It will be the glory that makes the difference.

After we left that day, the jail literally shook as the prisoners experienced deliverance from evil spirits and received the infilling of the Holy Spirit, evidenced by speaking in tongues. These are things that only the glory can do. The glory of God draws men and women unto Him. *Let the glory come!*

## THE CLOUD OF GLORY

I have seen the cloud of God's glory roll into the sanctuary of churches. It often presents as a haze or smoke, but usually comes in slowly, much as a natural cloud drifts. We've even seen a rainbow appear in the midst of the glory cloud. While ministering near Fort Lauderdale, Florida, I was sharing testimonies and talking about the supernatural when a cloud suddenly appeared, about three or four rows from the front. I have seen the cloud of God's glory many times, but never quite like this.

*"Pop! Pop!"* It exploded, and there it was. That cloud burst open above the people in that section. One second, nothing, and the next, there it was. A full, bright, puffy cloud shone over their heads. It was no more than five feet long, but everyone could see it.

Not long ago, I was ministering in Pensacola, Florida. During the first night of meetings, many people saw the cloud of glory appear as a haze in the atmosphere that could even be seen by those watching online. God's presence filled the room, and many people were blessed during that service. In that atmosphere, God did miracles among us in abundance.

The following night, the glory increased and, as it did, people felt the cloud's expansion. Miracles happened all over the room, including physical healings. Other signs of God's glory appeared. Many saw golden glory upon their hands, faces, and clothing. While I ministered, a large, golden hand print appeared on the back of my suit jacket. Some thought it was the hand of God. I personally believe it was the hand print of the miracle angel that travels with me everywhere I go. Regardless, the intensity of the glory that night was phenomenal.

At the end of the meeting, I gave an altar call for those who desired to receive Jesus Christ as their personal Lord and Savior. The altar area filled with people desiring to make first-time and renewed commitments to the Lord. The glory was thick. I ministered to many people. As the power of God touched them, people laid all over the floor.

Nobody wanted to leave when the meeting ended. Many stayed in the sanctuary and basked in the glory of God's presence. When the people finally left the church, the first thing they noticed was a thick cloud of smoke that had settled on the roof. God gave us another sign of His glory.

None of the other surrounding buildings had any cloud or fog resting upon them. Only the church was enveloped by the thick cloud which poured off it like a waterfall. People stood in the parking lot worshiping the Lord, and some took photos and videos of the manifestation. The glory increased. *Let the glory come!*

## WHEN THE GLORY COMES

*One thing I ask from the LORD, this only do I seek: that I may dwell in the house of the LORD all the days of my life, to gaze on the beauty of the LORD and to seek him in his temple.* (Psalm 27:4)

I've spent entire days weeping as the glory flooded my entire being with God's great love for the nations. At times, I've been so touched by the glory it became impossible to move, talk, or open my eyes. I've been caught up in trances and seen visions and the glories of heaven. In dreams, God showed me the people and places where I would minister, and the Spirit has carried me to those locations to be a blessing.

Embraced within the loving arms of God, I've felt His divine touch and tender kindness. I've known the whispers of His voice and been rendered speechless, unable to utter words to properly describe the things I had heard and seen. I've shaken for hours, trembling with holy reverence, as the glory moved throughout my entire being.

Like a fire, the work of God has burned within my soul. Angels cared for me, their wings fluttering with a refreshing Spirit breeze. Supernatural oil has flowed from my hands, and shimmering gold has fallen upon my head. As a witness to the signs of God's glory, I've been intoxicated on the new wine of His presence. I've found myself drunk for days with unspeakable joy that the world could never offer. His glory is everything. There have been times when I've worshiped for hours, and yet it felt like seconds. At other times, I've prophesied, worked miracles, spoken the messages given to my heart, and it was as though time stood still. In a matter of minutes the Spirit accomplished so much. The glory is eternal, and time must bend to its influence.

I've witnessed creative miracles happen in this realm: muscle growth on arms, the lengthening of legs, blind eyes opening to see, instant weight-loss coming on bodies, dental miracles, and diseases cured. Nothing is too difficult for the God of Glory.

THE INFLUENCE OF GOD'S GLORY SPREADS DEEP AND WIDE. THERE IS NO PLACE OR PERSON THE GLORY CANNOT REACH. THERE IS NO SITUATION WHERE THE GLORY CANNOT EXTEND ITS MIRACLE TOUCH.

Money appeared for us in unusual places or came to us in unusual ways. Hundreds, thousands, hundreds of thousands, and even millions of dollars are available for those who desire to seek the glory. There are no limitations in the glory realm. I've seen the spirit of poverty being broken over individuals and entire regions. The land was healed, as ungodly addictions were broken, mindsets changed, blessings spoken, and the curse reversed.

The influence of God's glory spreads deep and wide. There is no place or person the glory cannot reach. There is no situation where the glory cannot extend its miracle touch. The glory is the realm of highest power. *Let the glory come!*

Are you hungry to go deeper in the Spirit? He has greater things prepared for you as you determine to enter into these *Glory Realms*.

# PART II
# MOVING IN THE SUPERNATURAL

*"Not by might nor by power, but by my Spirit,"*
*says the* Lord *Almighty.*
—Zechariah 4:6

4

# REALMS OF DIVINE ASCENSION

*Who may ascend the mountain of the LORD?*
*Who may stand in his holy place?*
—Psalm 24:3

The question has been asked, *"Who may ascend the mountain of the LORD?"* Who are those who have found divine access into the glory realm? In the Scriptures, we read about the songs of ascents,[1] sometimes known as the songs of degrees, songs of steps, or pilgrim songs. Many scholars believe that these psalms were sung by Hebrew worshipers as they ascended the road to Zion to attend the three major feasts: Passover, Pentecost, and Tabernacles.[2] Herein, we discover the answer. Through the three realms of faith (Passover), anointing (Pentecost), and glory (Tabernacles), we're given progressive portals of entry to move higher and higher as we ascend the mountain of the Lord. When we travel in the spiritual mode of praise and worship, we accelerate in the Spirit, singing a new song.

God looks for worshipers who will worship in the Spirit and in truth (see John 4:23), as described in Psalm 24:4–5: *"The one who has clean hands and a pure heart, who does not trust in an idol or swear by a false god. They will receive blessing from the LORD."*

The Spirit gave us a divine pattern for entering into His manifest presence through praise and worship, laying it out so simply that anyone can embrace it. Ruth Ward Heflin was such an amazing woman of God and pioneer for us in the glory realm. In the early days of her ministry in Jerusalem, she felt prompted to worship on Mount Zion along with others who had come from the nations to seek the

Lord in His Holy City. During these extended times of worship, the Lord spoke prophetically to the group. It was from Mount Zion that Sister Ruth received a magnificent instruction from God: "Praise until the spirit of worship comes. Worship until the glory comes. Then stand in the glory."[3] It was profound yet just that easy.

There's a difference between praise, worship, and the glory. We need to learn about and understand the difference between them. Understanding and moving in all three is a heavenly pattern the Spirit gives every believer to enjoy. We move from praise into worship into manifest glory. We move from shouting into talking into intimate whispering. We move from outer court into the Holy Place into the Holy of Holies. We move from faith to anointing to glory. These are the three realms that concern us. All the parts work together to create a heavenly wheel that accommodates the presence of the Living God.

## OPENING THE DOOR FOR ENCOUNTER

> *"But now bring me a minstrel." And it came about, when the minstrel played, that the hand of the LORD came upon him.*
>
> (2 Kings 3:15 NASB)

Praise opens the door for us to ascend into the spiritual realm. We enter into God's presence with singing. (See Psalm 100:2.) In the protocol of the Spirit, praise is the key that unlocks the faith realm. (See verses 4–5.) That's why we find an emphasis on praise throughout the Scriptures. Music plays a major part in that praise:

> *Praise him with the sounding of the **trumpet**, praise him with the **harp** and **lyre**, praise him with **timbrel** and dancing, praise him with the **strings** and **pipe**, praise him with the **clash of cymbals**, praise him with **resounding cymbals**. Let everything that has **breath** praise the LORD.* (Psalm 150:3–6)

In the Bible, there are 1,028 references to music and more than two hundred verses encouraging us to sing. The longest book in the Bible, the Psalms, is actually God's songbook. There, and throughout the Scriptures, the Lord emphasized music, particularly in regards to releasing our new song. Singing is the language of the heart, and therefore also the language of the spirit. Praise and worship position us to connect Spirit to spirit.

God the Father sings (see Zephaniah 3:17), Jesus sings (see Hebrews 2:12), and the Holy Spirit sings (see Ephesians 5:19). Therefore, when the Spirit instructs us to sing, He is asking us to do what He does.

When music is performed horizontally, the earthly way, it can impress people or stir them emotionally. But when music is released vertically, the heavenly way, it attracts people to the overwhelming presence of God's glory and lifts them into that realm as well. As we sing God's praise, we synchronize with that glory vibration in the spirit world.

> SINGING IS THE LANGUAGE OF THE HEART, AND THEREFORE ALSO THE LANGUAGE OF THE SPIRIT. PRAISE AND WORSHIP POSITION US TO CONNECT SPIRIT TO SPIRIT.

Whenever new songs show up, new blessings always show up too. The Lord once spoke to me while in Dallas, Texas. He said, "Joshua, my mercies are new every morning. With every new day, there's a new song, and with every new song, there's a new glory." When I got that into my spirit, I realized that every single time I stand to praise the Lord, I must see Him as new to me that day. In the newness of God, a new song is to be sung. If I sing that new song, I come into and experience a glory I have never known before. When you do something you've never done, you get results you've never had. That's why the Scriptures encourage us to sing a new song.

## MUSIC AND HEALING

> *Whenever the spirit from God came on Saul, David would take up his lyre and play. Then relief would come to Saul; he would feel better, and the evil spirit would leave him.* (1 Samuel 16:23)

Music is able to break down barriers, open our minds, and soften our hearts. It also creates an atmosphere conducive for miracles. Traditional fields of medicine now use music to enhance learning, treat stress and pain, and bring healing.

Studies done on this subject have discovered that all pain and disease is a result of a lack of vibrational harmony in the body. Every organ, bone, and tissue of the body exists in a constant state of vibration. These vibrations within the body are the same frequencies found in musical tones, although the body resonates at a higher level of sound than the natural ear can hear.

Because music is a tool created by God to deliver healing power, the right kind of music can help the body come back into proper harmony. Under a microscope, cancer cells are disordered, scattered, and diffused, while healthy cells move harmoniously, with a proper sense of balance, alignment, and ease. (See the following diagram.)[4]

**Normal and Cancer Cells**
# Structure

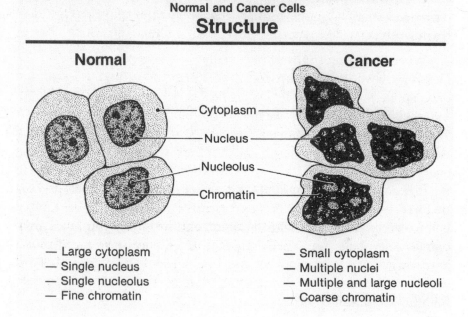

| Normal | Cancer |
|--------|--------|
| — Large cytoplasm | — Small cytoplasm |
| — Single nucleus | — Multiple nuclei |
| — Single nucleolus | — Multiple and large nucleoli |
| — Fine chromatin | — Coarse chromatin |

As we touch the glory of God's presence through our song, our body resonates in tune with the heavens. Our vibrational frequency is realigned with Jesus Christ.

Many times we have seen people completely healed by the power of God as they rested in the Spirit's presence during worship. What happened? The body came into alignment with heaven, the frequency of the body aligning itself with the frequency of glory, spirit connecting with Spirit.

During World War II, when musicians played for wounded servicemen, medics saw better healing results than in patients who were left to the quiet boredom of hospital life. Depression lessoned, expression increased, and contact with reality improved.[5]

Studies from the Harvard School of Medicine have shown that music assists in decreasing anxiety and patient discomfort, reduces side effects and levels of pain, accelerates the healing processes, improves the overall mood of patients, and aids in physical therapy and rehabilitation.[6] Music has also helped dissolve kidney stones, relieve knee pain, jaw pain (TMJ Syndrome), allergies, and more. The right kind of music—music filled with peace, presence, and glory—can literally bring the listener into a place of divine healing.

## THE SONG IN YOU

Scientists have discovered that your DNA contains a beautiful orchestral score.[7] Yes, your DNA contains a song. *You* are a song! The Scriptures instruct us to sing a new song to the Lord, and we are the song. He wants you to become a new song, a song filled with spirit and life.

If I came near you, I might not hear your song with my natural ear because it's on a different frequency. Have you ever been in a place where someone walked into the room, and instantly, you knew they carried a spiritual heaviness? Maybe it was sickness, a situation with a family member, or something else, but you could discern it. I believe we can pick up on others' songs that resonate at a higher auditory rate than we can naturally hear.

When your body is healthy, it puts out a vibrational frequency of health. However, when a spirit of sickness, with a frequency that's counter to your health, sets itself up in some portion of your body, it creates disharmony. Disharmony can be called dis-ease, or disease. Your body is no longer at ease.

But there is no dis-ease in the glory. The realm of the glory is a realm of ease. Therefore, no disease can exist in the glory. The Bible says that the power of life and death is in our tongue. The psalms encourage us to sing a new song to the Lord:

> *Deep calleth unto deep at the noise of thy waterspouts: all thy waves and thy billows are gone over me. Yet the LORD will command his lovingkindness in the daytime, and in the night his song shall be with me, and my prayer unto the God of my life.* (Psalm 42:7–8 KJV)

In order for our bodies to be in perfect harmony, we must come into alignment with the glory. Therefore, the Spirit's song must become our song.

## GOLD RECORDS FROM HEAVEN

One night, as I was ministering a revival in San Diego, the Spirit began speaking to me about submitting our "old records" to the flame of God, in order for Him to burn them, and then allowing Him to replace them with new "gold records" for His glory. I was reminded of the days of my youth when I would attend Christian summer camp, and we would always have one night during the week when the kids who were attending would take things that had become a bondage to them and throw them into a fire to be destroyed. Often, this would include ungodly record albums.

Now, God was inviting us to do the same thing, although in a spiritual sort of way. He was asking for our old records. You know, the ones that had become warped, gathered dust, and were covered in scratches. How many of these old broken records have we kept in our heart? They're old songs we've been playing over and over, hoping for a different atmosphere, records of deep pain, unforgiveness, sickness, poverty, abuse, disappointment, or false identity.

We must be honest with ourselves. Unfortunately, some of these records still exist in our massive collection from the past. We've allowed them to find a home in our heart, but the Spirit wants to change that. He wants to upgrade your sound, and replace all of your old records with new gold records from heaven. He wants to give you new sounds and new songs that will bring new successes. Even right now, ask the Spirit to take those old records and burn them in His all-consuming fire.

As I was ministering and sharing this revelation I was receiving, we actively began "pulling" these records from within (as though we were the jukeboxes), and we began prophetically throwing them into the fire. Great joy and freedom came in that very moment, as God was taking our old sounds and giving us His new sounds.

## SINGING THE NEW SONG

*Do not get drunk on wine, which leads to debauchery. Instead, be filled with the Spirit, speaking to one another with psalms, hymns, and songs from the Spirit. Sing and make music from your heart to the Lord, always giving thanks to God the Father for everything, in the name of our Lord Jesus Christ.* (Ephesians 5:18–20)

People have asked me how they might sing a new song if they're not musically talented or gifted in songwriting. I have good news: you don't need to be a professional musician in order to sing a new song. Just being willing to reach into the realms of faith, anointing, and glory brings the sounds of heaven into the earth. This requires a tolerance for change and a desire for more.

When we sing the new song, our spirit reaches out to connect with the Spirit of God, to know His heart, His will, His intention, and His words. We connect with Him, allowing the newness of God's words, which are spirit and life, to infiltrate our spirit, soul, and body.

The new song carries the potential to impart revelation, and the heart of God, into your heart. Sometimes this new song will be spontaneous because there's spontaneity in the glory of God, but this new song can also be structured and built with precision.

Often, when I worship the Lord, the new song flows, like a river from heaven. I can't see the beginning of it, and it has no end. I simply jump in at the point of reference that I've discovered. I splash around in this river. I swim in this river. I make new

> WHEN WE SING THE NEW SONG, OUR SPIRIT REACHES OUT TO CONNECT WITH THE SPIRIT OF GOD, TO KNOW HIS HEART, HIS WILL, HIS INTENTION, AND HIS WORDS.

discoveries in the river and enjoy the refreshment that the river brings. Sometimes, I ponder these moments later during my devotion time with the Lord. Sometimes, the song continues to come up from my spirit for days. When that happens, I recognize the special touch of glory that is upon these words and music.

Sometimes the touch of God is the rhythm and timing of the sound. When this happens, I sit down and work through what God is saying to me. Usually, it comes piece by piece and layer by layer. Always remember that revelation is progressive. God is building something inside of us.

Regardless of when, where, or how it comes, the new song is always fresh because it's inspired by the Spirit. This sound pushes back barriers and moves mountains, and yet, at the same time, can also sound familiar. At times, God anoints the old hymns with a new sound, and they become an entirely new song.

Many times while I'm leading worship, God drops a word or two into my spirit. We may be singing a song and God emphasizes a particular phrase or sentence from that song. This is where we need to be sensitive to the prompting and direction of the Holy Spirit, the best musical director of all time. I will pick up that word or phrase and sing it over and over, in accordance with what the Spirit highlights.

One time we were singing the old church hymn, "Nothing but the Blood of Jesus." A new awareness and revelation of the blood came into the midst of the congregation. You could feel it swirling, and I began singing a new song:

> It's the blood.
> It's the blood.
> It's the blood.
> It's the blood of Jesus.

We sang that one phrase over and over. God was using it to impart something special into our lives. We were connected with the heart and sacrifice of God as we moved to worship the Lord in this way. We were worshiping with heaven.

God brought this new song into the middle of an old hymn, so don't be surprised where or when God brings these new songs to you. Don't underestimate the power of the new song and what it can do in the hearts of people and yourself. And don't dismiss something because it's old or has been done before. God may want to revive the old bones with His breath that breathes through you.

While ministering in Osaka, Japan, I heard the worshipers playing their instruments using the ancient pentatonic scale (a familiar oriental sound). I felt the pleasure of God on this music and heard the Spirit say, "There is an ancient praise for the Ancient of Days. It's an old sound that's becoming a new song." This revelation delighted me. God wants to redeem ancient sounds and instruments and bring them forth with new songs in our day. I believe this is one of the keys God will use to restore nations in His glory.

Be open to the moving of God's Spirit when it comes to singing the new song. If you are, the Lord will use you to advance into new territory. The new song is everywhere and is available for all who have ears ready to hear and mouths ready to sing.

I want to give you three keys for opening yourself to singing the new song. If you put these into practice, you will find yourself in a new realm of glory.

## 1. MAKE MUSIC IN YOUR HEART

In Ephesians 5:18, we are instructed to be filled with the Spirit, which happens as we sing songs from the Spirit. Actually, this is a reciprocal instruction. I've discovered that those who are filled with the Spirit spontaneously praise as a natural response to being filled. The Spirit gives you His sounds, rhythms, and songs. The key is to allow that song to come forth from your spirit.

> WHEN YOU RELEASE THE SOUND GOD PLACES IN YOUR HEART, IT WILL OPEN UP AN ENTIRELY NEW REALM INTO THE SUPERNATURAL.

Don't be afraid to hum, whistle, or sing the melody that the Spirit places within you. When you first recognize it, it will come without words. You might sing "la-la-la" or "do-do-do," but God will take that melody and use it in a supernatural way. I like to sing first thing in the morning while getting ready for the day, but you can sing in your car on the way to work or while walking down the street. The Scriptures encourage us to make music from our heart unto the Lord, and that's the important thing. When you release the sound God places in your heart, it will open up an entirely new realm into the supernatural.

## 2. SING IN THE SPIRIT

We find the next step for singing the new song in 1 Corinthians 14:15: *"So what shall I do? I will pray with my spirit, but I will also pray with my understanding; I will sing with my spirit, but I will also sing with my understanding."* Some people have read this Scripture and come to the conclusion that it's more important to pray and sing with their understanding than praying and singing in the Spirit. That is the wrong perspective.

Recognize that everything begins in the Spirit. We cannot properly pray with our own understanding. It is the Spirit who gives us insight into the thoughts and intents of God. Singing is the same. We must do it first in the Spirit. Once you make melody in your heart, sing that tune in the Spirit. If you haven't yet received your prayer language, I would encourage you to read my book, *Simple Supernatural*,[8] and allow me to pray with you to receive the baptism in the Holy Spirit, as evidenced by speaking in tongues. Then, sing in the Spirit and allow the Spirit of God to sing through you.

## 3. SING WITH YOUR UNDERSTANDING

The final step to singing the new song is to transition from singing in the Spirit to singing with your natural understanding. You may be amazed by what the Lord has been speaking through you when you translate your song in this way. There have been times when I've sung over nations and other times when the new song comes forth as a simple declaration over my personal life.

We've sung the new song corporately, discovering that each of us held a special portion of the song. When we released it together, God painted the larger picture for us. Your new song can flow with healing, it can flow as a prophetic word, and it can come forth with great encouragement.

Don't worry if your new song seems simple. The things of God are simple enough for a child to understand. Sophistication is not a requirement when singing the new song. Let the Spirit of God flow through you and bring forth His glory.

## THE HIGH PRAISES OF GOD

God looks for us to give Him a *high* praise. The high praise can only come from the high place! So, we must ascend. Psalm 149:6 (KJV) says, *"Let the high praises of God be in their mouth, and a two-edged sword in their hand."* What does that mean? When God's Word becomes your word and the high praises become your praise, you no longer speak on your own. Instead, you speak what God has spoken. With His Word in your mouth, God speaks through you. When the two of you speak together, the words become a double-edged sword.

What does that double-edged sword do? It destroys and tears down the words of the enemy. It annihilates whatever the enemy has set up against you, and every attack the enemy has tried to bring against your life. As the Lord's song becomes your song, you move into complete and total victory.

## PRAISE CHANGES THE ATMOSPHERE

> *Yet you are enthroned as the Holy One; you are the one Israel praises.* (Psalm 22:3)

This verse doesn't just say that God *abides* in our praises; it says He is actually *enthroned upon* our praises. Within our praise, God finds a throne, a place where He can rule and reign.

Praise is acknowledging God for what He has done, what He is doing, and what He is going to do. It comes from the Hebrew word *halal*, which means "to shine; hence, to make a show, to boast; and thus to be (clamorously) foolish; to rave; causatively, to celebrate." Praise is a verb, an action word, and every time we set out to praise the Lord, action should be involved.

We praise God with our dance, our shout, our joyful songs, and our clapping. We use musical instruments and our voices to make His praise loud. Because action is involved with our praise, it changes the atmosphere. Your praise takes you past where you've been and gives you spiritual movement to ascend higher.

We praise God for what He *has done* (that's the past), for what He *is doing* (that's the present), and for what He *is going to do* (that's the future). I like telling people that I'm not praising because of what I'm going *through*, but because of where I'm going *to*. This puts us in motion to move farther up the mountain of the Lord.

Corporate praise brings forth corporate worship, which leads us into corporate glory. This is the greater glory. You might think you're the only one who wants to praise God in this way, but step out in boldness and invite others to join you. Often, when we are in a congregational praise setting, Janet and I invite those around us to join hands with us, so we can corporately dance together in the altar area. Some refuse, but there are always those who were just waiting for the invitation.

> CORPORATE PRAISE BRINGS FORTH CORPORATE WORSHIP, WHICH LEADS US INTO CORPORATE GLORY. THIS IS THE GREATER GLORY.

We like to make what we call "praise waves." This is when you join hands and dance forward and backward, making a wave across the front of the church. You may start with only two or three, but soon others will engage and participate as you step out in faith to ascend the mountain. At other times, we may form a train, dancing around the perimeter of the sanctuary, or make circles that form wheels within wheels. Whatever we do, we dance together in joy.

Listen to what God speaks through the words of the song, and prophetically move into action. If you're singing about the open door, then take a step through it. If you're singing about the river, jump and splash in its waters. If you're singing about going higher, reach into that realm and see yourself in that higher sphere.

Praise is the voice of faith. When you praise, God gives you faith to receive the promise. Your praise takes you where no one else's praise can. That's why you must express yourself through praise. The greater we express ourselves in praise, the greater we extend ourselves in worship. Our praise changes the atmosphere, but worship takes us further.

## WORSHIP CARRIES US FURTHER

Worship is acknowledging God for who He is. Worship is different from praise. In worship, we move from a place of acknowledging God's acts and what He has done or what He is going to do, into a place of recognizing who He is and honoring Him. The Hebrew word for worship is *shachah*, which means "to bow down." The Greek word *proskuneo* means "to kiss the hand toward one, in token of reverence." Worship, then, is honoring and bowing down before our God with reverence.

True worship, however, is really an issue of the heart and soul rather than a physical action or position. Jesus said that worship is done in vain when: *"Their **hearts** are far from me"* (Matthew 15:8). Worship causes us to draw near to the throne. (See Hebrews 10:22.)

We worship Him because He's holy.

We worship Him because He's worthy.

The Lord deserves our worship, and there should always be a sense of ascending when we worship Him. If you're not moving during worship, then you're not really worshiping—you're just singing a song. Worship moves us toward Him and away from worldly distractions.

When Jesus met the Samaritan woman at the well, He said to her:

*Believe me, a time is coming when you will worship the Father neither on this mountain nor in Jerusalem. You Samaritans worship what you do not know; we worship what we do know, for salvation is from the Jews. Yet a time is coming and has now come when the true worshipers will worship the Father in the Spirit and in truth, for*

*they are the kind of worshipers the Father seeks. God is spirit, and his*
*worshipers must worship in the Spirit and in truth.*

(John 4:21–24)

The Samaritans worshiped on a sacred mountain, but Jesus challenged this woman to a new kind of worship. God was not looking for
a worshiper on an earthly mountain, but for someone who would worship Him from another location—a spiritual mountain, in the spirit
and in truth.

We must be led by the Spirit to ascend the mountain of the Lord.
John the Revelator was *"in the Spirit"* (see Revelation 1:10–18) when he
saw a vision of God's throne. In this vision, John received great clarity and revelatory detail regarding the Lordship of Christ. He heard
Jesus's voice (see Revelation 1:10) and saw Him seated on the throne
(see Revelation 1:13).

If we want to worship accurately, we must worship in the Spirit.
Our song must move from an earthly perspective to a heavenly one.
Praise moves us past our feelings by faith, moves us past any disappointments, and past the limitations of the natural. Praise connects
us to a supernatural flow in the Spirit. Worship carries us into God's
heart. It's the connection between the praise realm and the glory
realm.

In the early days of ministry, I was flowing in worship one evening
during a time of altar ministry. Suddenly, the Spirit lifted me into a
higher dimension. It's difficult to describe with earthly words the way
it all happened.

As I sang in the Spirit, it was as if my entire being vibrated with
that sound and I became a worship unto the Lord. In that moment, I
felt lighter than air, my spirit-man enlarged beyond the capacity of
my physical body. When my body could no longer hold my spirit, I
ascended into the glory.

This was something new for me. Even though my physical body
remained at the keyboard, my hands still playing the piano, my spirit-man was taken up. I floated above myself and was fully aware of
God's heart and intentions for those present at the meeting.

In the Spirit, I saw clearly. Nothing was hidden. I knew that the Spirit wanted to heal every person who was broken, and cleanse every place that was defiled. His love for everyone in that room was undeniable. But more than anything, God wanted a true, intimate relationship with each person there, spirit to Spirit.

In that encounter, God spoke many things to me, but He didn't need words to communicate His thoughts. That's why it's so difficult to speak about or try to explain these things in the natural. When they happen, they happen in the Spirit, and in the Spirit, there is perfect understanding.

In that realm, you know even as you are known, the confinements of the flesh no longer a burden or a barrier to communication. This is why we must worship until the glory comes, because in the glory there is a knowing. We become much more useful when we synchronize with the purposes of heaven.

## HOW THE REALMS OF PRAISE AND WORSHIP WORK TOGETHER

Praise is loud and exuberant. We dance and jump. We acknowledge what God has done, is doing, and will do. In comparison, worship is intimate. We don't dance and jump, but lift our hands and speak intimately with our Lord.

In worship, we acknowledge who He is. He is Lord. He is the Healer. He is our Savior. He is everything we need. In the glory, we stand in holy stillness.

When we move into the glory through our praise and worship, miracles happen automatically, without much effort on our part. We simply see what God is doing in praise, and honor His presence in worship. He responds to us in glory. All successful miracle ministries understand this simple principle, that music creates an atmosphere. We must understand that the realm of praise and worship opens up another dimension for us—the dimension of the glory. When the glory comes in, you no longer strive or struggle for miracles. When the glory realm comes, it brings an ease, and, as you stand in that realm, the fullness of God encompasses your life.

| In Praise | In Worship | In Glory |
|---|---|---|
| *We express ourselves.* | *We extend ourselves.* | *We yield ourselves.* |
| *We are loud and exuberant.* | *We draw near to God.* | *We stand in holy stillness.* |
| *We dance and jump, celebrating God's goodness.* | *We lift our hands, recognizing God's majestic greatness.* | *We connect, spirit to Spirit.* |
| *We acknowledge what He has done, what He is doing, and what He will continue to do!* | *We acknowledge who He is.* | *We receive divine revelation and heavenly perspective.* |
| **Outer Court** | **Holy Place** | **Holy of Holies** |
| **Faith** | **Anointing** | **Manifest Presence** |
| **Passover** | **Pentecost** | **Tabernacles** |

## STANDING IN THE GLORY

*I have seen you in the sanctuary and beheld your power and your glory.* (Psalm 63:2)

When you praise, don't stop until you reach the realms of worship, and when you worship, don't stop until you reach the realms of glory. As you attain this, you bring the atmosphere of the heavenly cloud into your midst. Feel the cloud, see the cloud, sense the cloud, hear the cloud, and experience the cloud. Many times in the midst of worship, my vision was suddenly changed. All I could see was the cloud and God's glory. I knew other worshipers were still around me, but I couldn't see them. As I stood in that posture of seeing the glory, I gave all my attention to the purposes of God. He speaks to us in the thickness of the cloud, and we hear His voice with clarity. Although it may not be audible to the natural ear, learn how to wait and listen in the glory.

At other times, as the cloud came upon us in worship, I've lifted my hands into the air and felt the weight of the manifestation. In agreement, I've touched the cloud and received the blessings that come from that glory. Once you experience the cloud, all things are possible in that realm and that dimension—the glory realm.

Even in Old Testament times, when musicians and singers worshiped together in one accord, their music created an atmosphere in which God revealed Himself through the cloud of His glory:

> It came even to pass, as the trumpeters and singers were as one, to make one sound to be heard in praising and thanking the LORD, and when they lifted up their voice with the trumpets and cymbals and instruments of musick, and praised the LORD, saying: For He is good, For His mercy endureth for ever: that then the house was filled with a cloud, even the house of the LORD; So that the priests could not stand to minister by reason of the cloud: for the glory of the LORD had filled the house of God. (2 Chronicles 5:13–14 KJV)

Capture this revelation in your spirit: the glory of the Lord filled the house of God. What is the glory? As we noted in the last chapter, God is the glory, and the glory is God. But the glory is also a place. Because God is the glory, the realm where He dwells is the glory realm. As we are surrounded and possessed by this glory realm, every fiber of our body responds to that glory. This is why it's so important for us to come into a place of praise and then worship so that we can move on into the glory.

We should never just praise, and then stop. We should never just worship, and then stop. The ultimate goal of our praise and worship is complete surrender to the glory realm of God. Only in the glory are we eternally changed. Only by the power of His glory can we experience the difference, a divine shift in our life, and miracles begin to flow. This is an important foundation upon which you need to operate, not to see occasional signs and wonders in your life, but to live continuously in a dimension of the miraculous. In the glory, miracles will take place all around you, all the time.

ONLY IN THE GLORY ARE WE ETERNALLY CHANGED. ONLY BY THE POWER OF HIS GLORY CAN WE EXPERIENCE THE DIFFERENCE, A DIVINE SHIFT IN OUR LIFE, AND MIRACLES BEGIN TO FLOW.

Medical science is exploring a concept they call cellular memory. They have discovered that the cells of your body have a mind or a memory within them that can recall events, atmospheres, and actions that took place in the past. Your cells remember. This is why making time to stand in the glory is so essential. Too many people rush through praise and worship as though it were a preliminary event, not recognizing that God's glory is everything. Without it, we cannot do what we're created to do. It's in these moments of glory that we are forever changed, even down to the cellular level.

Science is just beginning to notice and understand these things, but thousands of years ago, the psalmist David sang about his inward longing for the essence of God's presence: *"How lovely is your dwelling place, LORD Almighty! My soul yearns, even faints, for the courts of the LORD; my heart and my flesh cry out for the living God"* (Psalm 84:1–2).

As a teenager, my life changed forever in a moment of glory. Although I was raised in a loving Christian home, it was within the depths of the cloud that I received a zeal and passion for the things of God. Learning how to stand in the glory changed me forever. Vision comes in this realm, as the purposes of God become all we see. As we stand in the glory, we are lifted to new levels of knowing the Spirit.

The diagram below shows how these three realms move us upward within the whirlwind of the Spirit.

As we praise and worship the Lord, we posture ourselves for the fullness of this glory to come, with all of its miracle possibilities, blessings, and heavenly hosts of angels. Our worship attracts angelic presence. I want you to see how you can open these realms further as we keeping moving in the glory.

Are you hungry to go deeper in the Spirit? He has greater things prepared for you as you determine to enter into these *Glory Realms*.

# 5

# REALMS OF ANGELIC PRESENCE

*There is rejoicing in the presence of the angels of God.*
—Luke 15:10

**W**here there is glory, there are angels, and where there are angels, there is glory. You can't separate them. These realms are intertwined with each other.

If you look throughout the Scriptures, you find angels available to saints in days gone by. But the Scriptures also give us a clear understanding of the ways we can engage with angels in present times.

As a young child, I was very aware of this dimension. I played with my angels in the backyard and often saw them worshiping the Lord when at church. Unfortunately, some adults told me it was wrong to see or talk about what I was experiencing. Being a child, I listened to them, and that supernatural realm closed to me for many years. It wasn't until my early twenties that this realm was reawakened for me through a dream.

## MEETING MY ANGELS

*He had a dream in which he saw a stairway resting on the earth, with its top reaching to heaven, and the angels of God were ascending and descending on it.* (Genesis 28:12)

In my dream, I was lifted into an ethereal sphere above the earth where I encountered three of my guardian angels. They introduced themselves to me and explained their purpose and ministry functions in my life.

The first angel told me he'd been assigned to release creative miracles, signs, and wonders wherever I ministered. He was also to operate in bringing me unusual gifts and blessings from heaven.

The second angel told me he would administrate the new songs and the flow of heaven's sound in my life. He was an angel of praise and worship.

The third angel said that he had been assigned to release holy boldness and strength into my life during times of timidity. Something unusual had happened to me in these three areas, and this explained it. These things exploded in me.

What struck me most about those huge angelic beings was their appearance. They wore brilliant robes, just like the angels I had seen as a child. But these angels looked just like me! They were much taller and broader. Each one had a distinct hairstyle. Their eye color swirled with heaven's beauty. But they looked like my angelic brothers.

Through this encounter, I realized the importance of the relationship of angels to humanity. After that experience, I researched these amazing spiritual beings, pursued them in the Scriptures, and positioned myself for further revelations regarding their activities. Since that time, the presence of angels continues to increase in my life and ministry. Often, when we get into the glory realm in a corporate meeting, I sense their involvement in the ministry that follows.

## SPIRITUAL GUARDIANS

Angels are assigned as spiritual guardians and protectors over your life, and many Scriptures confirm this. Some still ask, "Do we really have guardian angels?" Yes, we do. There have been a lot of theological discussions about whether or not each of us has a guardian angel. What I read about this subject in the Word of God convinces me of their presence.

Psalm 91:11–12, for example, says, *"For he will command his angels concerning you to guard you in all your ways; they will lift you up in their hands, so that you will not strike your foot against a stone."* In other words, angels protect you—it is God's assignment. Since angels are for our protection, it follows to call them "guardian angels."

Psalm 34:7 says, *"The angel of the LORD encamps around those who fear him, and he delivers them."* Matthew 18:10 clearly speaks about their relationship to children saying, *"See that you do not despise one of these little ones. For I tell you that their angels in heaven always see the face of my Father in heaven."* Jesus Himself told us, *"these little ones,"* these children, had guardian angels. Therefore, we should not be found guilty of looking down on them.

Like the angels I encountered in my dream, guardian angels look like the person to whom they are assigned. Some years ago, I made this statement in a meeting in Virginia. A woman came to me afterward and said, "You know that's in the Bible." I didn't. She related the story of when Peter supernaturally escaped from prison, he went to Mary's house where the early church was gathered. They thought it was his angel at the door instead of Peter himself. (See Acts 12:6–15.) I had read this passage of Scripture many times, but hadn't noticed that part of it before. That happens to us sometimes.

Another time, while ministering in Albuquerque, New Mexico, Pastor Mary Dorian said to me, "I see an angel with you here in the meeting, and he looks just like you." How wonderful when others see into the realm of the Spirit and confirm what we have seen! I believe the things I am discussing in this book will also bring confirmation to you regarding things you've experienced in the Spirit. God wants to open these realms for you more and more.

## OTHER IMPORTANT TRUTHS ABOUT THE ANGELIC REALM

Angels are mentioned at least 108 times in the Old Testament and 165 times in the New Testament. Ample scriptural evidence exists, allowing us to build a foundation for our basic knowledge of angelic beings.

The word *angel* is translated from the Greek word *aggelos*, which means "messenger" or "sent one." The Hebrew word *mal'ak* has the same meaning. These two words occur almost three hundred times within the Scriptures.

According to the dictionary, angels are "a class of spiritual beings; celestial attendants of God." According to Christian tradition, angels constitute the lowest of the nine celestial orders, consisting of three specific realms (again correlating with the three realms in the Spirit). Angels are intricately involved in the work of God on the earth. They encircle the life of the believer. Every individual is assigned at least one angel from birth. (See Psalm 91:11.)

Angels are spiritual beings created by God to serve Him. Therefore, they have not existed from all eternity. (See Nehemiah 9:6; Psalm 148:2, 5.)

Colossians 1:16–17 (NASB) explains:

*For by Him all things were created, both in the heavens and on earth, visible and invisible, whether thrones or dominions or rulers or authorities—all things have been created through Him and for Him. He is before all things, and in Him all things hold together.*

The timing of the creation of angels is not specified, but most likely occurred in connection with the creation of the heavens in Genesis 1:1. God may have created the angels immediately after He created the heavens but before He created the earth. According to Job 38:7: *"All the angels shouted for joy"* when He laid the foundations of the earth.

> ANGELS ARE INTRICATELY INVOLVED IN THE WORK OF GOD ON THE EARTH. THEY ENCIRCLE THE LIFE OF THE BELIEVER.

Faithful angels have remained obedient to God and continue to carry out His will. Others, fallen angels, disobeyed, fell from their holy position, and now operate in active opposition to the work and plan of God.

Consider these truths from the Scriptures concerning angels:

- Angels are never to be worshiped. Never pray to an angel; never bow down to an angel. The Scriptures are clear about this. (See Colossians 2:18; Revelation 19:10; 22:9.)

- Angels are immortal and have great strength, but are not omnipotent. Angels do not need rest or sleep. They can work, work, work, work, and work some more. They were created that way to be spirit messengers, spirit helpers, and ministers that never tire.

- Angels are commonly seen in large numbers, as the Bible speaks about a *multitude* of angels or a *great host* of angels. I like what Hebrews 12:22 says, *"But you have come to Mount Zion, to the city of the living God, the heavenly Jerusalem. You have come to thousands upon thousands of angels in joyful assembly."* Angels are in *joyful assembly*. Did you know that angels are happy, they are joyful, and there are thousands upon thousands of them? That's amazing!

- Angels are not glorified human beings. Matthew 22:30 explains that they do not marry or reproduce like humans. Hebrews 12:22–23 (NASB) says that when we get to the heavenly Jerusalem, we will be met by *"myriads of angels"* and *"the spirits of righteous made perfect"*—two separate groups, the latter being a part of the great cloud of witnesses. (See Hebrews 12:1.) Angels are a company of spiritual beings, not a race descended from a common ancestor. (See Luke 20:34–36.) We are called "sons of men," but angels are never called "sons of angels."

- Most angelic beings do not have wings. The seraphim and cherubim do have wings. Several biblical passages picture angels with wings (see Isaiah 6:2, 6), while other verses talk about angels flying. (We assume wings would be useful for flight.) (See Daniel 9:21.) Still, it's possible for angels to move about without depending on wings. When I was very young, I remember seeing angels flying around the ceiling of the church sanctuary, yet I don't remember them having any visible wings. Dressed in sparkling white robes, they took on the appearance of large men. Most references to angels in the Bible say nothing about wings. In passages like Genesis chapters 18 and 19, it is certain that no wings were visible at all.

- Some angels can't be trusted. As author Brenda Redmond has noted, "The Bible classifies some angels as *elect* (see 1 Timothy 5:21) or *holy* (see Matthew 25:31; Mark 8:38). Although all angels were originally holy, enjoying the presence of God (see Matthew 18:10) and the environment of heaven (see Mark 13:32), other angels opposed God, choosing the leadership of Lucifer (see Matthew 25:41; 2 Peter 2:4; Jude 6; Ephesians 6:12)."[1] We call these dark angels *demons* and must be careful to not be deceived if they appear in our lives. According to the Scriptures, we don't need to be fearful of these unholy angels. Instead, we take authority over them in the name of Jesus and cast them out. (See Mark 16:17; Luke 10:19.)

## THE NATURE OF ANGELS

- Unlike human beings, angels do not have permanent physical bodies. They are spirit beings with personal spirit bodies. Jesus declared, *"A spirit does not have flesh and bones as you see that I have"* (Luke 24:39 ESV). Most often angels appear in dazzling, white, shimmer and blazing glory. (See Matthew 28:2–4.)

- Because they consist of Spirit and light, angels are capable, at the very least, of traveling at the speed of light the fastest speed known to man. Light travels 186,282 miles per second, and the circumference of the earth is only 24,901 miles. This means it's possible for angels to travel completely around the world seven and a half times in just one second. This gives an idea of how quickly they can move, minister, and accomplish God's purposes in the earth.

- Although angels can move at record speeds, the Scriptures make it clear they can only be in one place at a time. They must have a localized presence and are not omnipresent.

- Angels receive assignments. When assigned to a situation, they dedicate themselves to that situation.

- Angels can take on the appearance of either men or women, as the occasion demands. (See Zechariah 5:9.) How else would it be possible to *"entertain angels unaware"* (Hebrews 13:2)? They can also manifest in various sizes (see Revelation 7:1), physical forms, including animal likenesses (see 2 Kings 2:11–12; 6:13–17; Zechariah 1:8–11; Ezekiel, chapters 1 and 10), and spiritual dimensions such as visions, trances, and dreams.

Several years ago, a group of angels showed up at one of my meetings. They were dressed in hospital scrubs, taking on an appearance like that of doctors or nurses. Each of them had what appeared to be an intravenous drip, but instead of there being medicine inside the bag, their IVs were filled with new wine. The Spirit gave me an understanding that these angels had been sent into the meeting to minister to various individuals in a peculiar way. The new wine was filled with healing heavenly provision and the life of the Spirit. Although it may seem unusual, I have become aware of these angels a few times since that initial encounter. Whenever I see them, I mention it to those who are present, because oftentimes, those angels have been sent to minister directly to those people. If you recognize the appearance of the angelic, you can participate with it.

## THE NAMES OF ANGELS

*Manoah said to the angel of the LORD, "What is your name, so that when your words come to pass, we may honor you?" But the angel of the LORD said to him, "Why do you ask my name, seeing it is wonderful?"* (Judges 13:17–18 NASB)

There are many different names used when speaking about angels in the Scriptures, each name reflecting a specific function and purpose:

- Daniel called them *"watchers."* (See Daniel 10:13.)
- Jacob called them *"God's host."* (See Genesis 32:2.)
- The psalmist David called them *"holy ones."* (See Psalm 89:7.)
- Job called them *"the sons of God."* (See Job 1:6; Job 38:7.)
- To Abraham, they were *"three men."* (See Genesis 18:2.)

And the list goes on.

In ancient cultures, names revealed something important about a person or their lineage. Biblical names usually give us a clue as to some characteristic or function of the bearer's name. If that's also true for angels, it's natural to want to know the names of your personal angels.

As we have seen in Judges 13, Manoah inquired of the angel about his name, and he responded by telling him it was Wonderful. I've met people who were introduced to angels named Revival and Healing, and that was exactly what their ministry function was.

I remember ministering at a church in Sonora, California, near Yosemite National Park. One night, another minister came and told me he was accompanied by an angel named Breakthrough. Sure enough, in the meeting the evidence of that angelic ministry was obvious. An explosion of miracles, signs, and wonders, and a massive spiritual breakthrough was released over the entire region. All these years later, I still meet people once in a while who testify about what happened during those meetings.

My personal angels have told me their names, which are connected to their eternal purpose. If you have the opportunity, ask your angels their names and listen for the answer. Through doing this, you may learn more about their specific function and ministry operation in your life.

## THE THREE-FOLD PURPOSE OF ANGELS

The Spirit is shedding new light on this all-important subject, showing us the parts of His Word that deal with the angelic realm. It is because now, more than ever, we need the glory of God to be present in our everyday situations.

According to the Scriptures, angels serve a three-fold purpose in our lives: to acclaim, to act, and to assist. I like to call these *The Three A's of Angelic Ministry*. Everything angels do is based upon those three A's.

### TO ACCLAIM *GOD*

Angels always direct praise and worship to God, never to themselves. They want to see others worship God alone and lift Him up in their lives:

*You alone are the LORD. You made the heavens, even the highest heavens, and all their starry host, the earth and all that is on it, the seas and all that is in them. You give life to everything, and the multitudes of heaven worship you.* (Nehemiah 9:6)

### TO ACT *IN SPIRITUAL COMBAT*

Angels wage war on our behalf. They fight in the battle between right and wrong and hold up God's standard of truth. Many times, these battles happen behind the scenes in the spiritual dimension and are unknown to us. This is a battle that belongs to the Lord, so you can rest in the blessing that belongs to you as an heir of salvation. *"Then war broke out in heaven. Michael and his angels fought against the dragon, and the dragon and his angels fought back"* (Revelation 12:7).

## TO OTHERWISE ASSIST MANKIND

Angels intervene in the daily lives of people on the earth. According to the Scriptures, they are God's servants and assist the heirs of salvation to fulfill their eternal callings. *"Are not all angels ministering spirits sent to serve those who will inherit salvation?"* (Hebrews 1:14)

There will be days ahead when the only way we will be able to survive is by the Spirit's supernatural intervention. That includes the ministering angels that God has assigned to our life, a provision He has made available for us from heaven.

We all need the supernatural. That's why my wife Janet and I have been led to train students at the International Glory Institute with both live and online teachings. We are continually raising up students who know how to operate in the supernatural realm. The angels are at your service, to assist you with God's purposes for your life, but you must learn how to activate them, how to engage with this realm.

## THE ANGELS OF THE NATIONS

Not only are angels available to assist us in our personal lives, but God has also created angels that interact in the affairs of countries. At one of the International Glory Institutes we conducted in Palm Springs, California, a group of people came early. As they prayed and interceded while walking through the meeting room and hallways of the facility, they saw the angels of the nations come in and gather in preparation for the school. I believe in these angels, and, even when I don't see them, I trust they are present when we meet to conduct one of our schools of ministry, for people from many nations attend those gatherings. These angels are present to stand watch and listen, intent upon hearing the words that will be declared or decreed in such a meeting. Then they will be dispatched to bring those words to pass.

My first encounter with the angels of the nations was at the Town Hall in Pukekohe, in the Auckland region of New Zealand. It was our final meeting of a month-long ministry trip, and we had invited many leaders to gather with us for a special time of intercession.

As the night progressed, I saw angels gathering around the room. They were lined up, shoulder to shoulder, around the entire inside perimeter of the Town Hall auditorium. I immediately knew they were the angels of the nations, because not only were they filled with light, but also were dressed in the garments of the nations they represented.

I was astonished by the presence of these angels and wondered why they were there. Then I realized that we were praying for different nations and making declarations concerning them. These angels came to listen to the decrees being spoken over the nations of North America, Africa, South America, Asia, the Middle East, Australasia, and Europe—all the different parts of the world. The angels listened attentively. Once they heard our declarations, they took them back to those nations and implemented them.

The glory was very strong in those meetings. Pastor Joye Johnson's mother, Mrs. Mellor, who was well into her eighties at the time, said the spiritual intensity compared to her memories of attending Smith Wigglesworth's meetings in Wellington when she was seven-years-old. The entire experience was quite phenomenal, to say the least.

## EVEN JESUS NEEDED THE MINISTRY OF ANGELS

Jesus knew the cross was coming and needed to prepare for it. (See Luke 22:41–43.) While Jesus prayed in the garden of Gethsemane, God sent an angel to help Him. The Father could have come Himself and strengthened Jesus, or Jesus could have received supernatural power in another way. But the Bible makes it clear that Jesus received strength through the ministry of an angel.

When Jesus lived here on earth, He served as our greatest example. He said that we would do what He had done, and even *"greater things than these"* (John 14:12). So, not only will we live as Jesus lived, but our connection to heaven will be greater. The manifestation of God's power in us would be increased. If angels ministered to Jesus, I believe we can expect that God will send angels to minister to us. He desires us to experience the activation of and interaction with the angelic realm.

## ANGELS BRING US JOY

*But the angel said to them, "Do not be afraid. I bring you good news that will cause great joy for all the people."*     (Luke 2:10)

While we were ministering in Cardiff, Wales, joy angels came into the meeting and holy laughter broke out. All over the congregation, the people laughed spontaneously. One fellow was turned upside down in his seat. His head rested on the floor, his feet stuck up in the air, and he kept laughing hysterically. Angels had come on the scene to minister the joy of the Lord to His people. We've seen this happen in many places as we've learned how to cooperate with the angels that bring great joy.

What is the purpose of this? We've seen people suffering from long-term depression become ecstatic about life again. Those who experienced terrible abuse and trauma were restored by the joy of the Lord. It became a supernatural strength for them.

## ANGELS DELIVER MIRACLES AND REVELATION

There are angels that direct preachers, giving clear direction or instruction from God. Where does this revelation come from? From God, and God alone. The angel is only the messenger, the delivery service. We must understand that difference. We're not receiving revelation from an angel; we're receiving revelation from God.

Angels are messengers and deliver miracles. Angels don't do the miracles. They deliver them. They're not originating the revelation; they're delivering the revelation. We must understand the difference. God uses angelic ministry in the same way we use FedEx. The angel is just a delivery agent who brings us revelation.

> ANGELS DON'T DO THE MIRACLES. THEY DELIVER THEM. THEY'RE NOT ORIGINATING THE REVELATION; THEY'RE DELIVERING THE REVELATION.

This was true in the Old Testament, true during Jesus's time, true during the period of the early church, and is still true today. As an example, Paul traveled on a ship that encountered a severe storm:

*After they had gone a long time without food, Paul stood up before them and said: "Men, you should have taken my advice not to sail from Crete; then you would have spared yourselves this damage and loss. But now I urge you to keep up your courage, because not one of you will be lost; only the ship will be destroyed."* (Acts 27:21–22)

These men probably wondered how he could say such a thing, how he could know that not one of them would be lost. Paul did say that the ship would be destroyed. Those are very strange circumstances. A ship lost, but none of its passengers harmed.

Paul went on to explain how he knew all of this:

*Last night an angel of the God to whom I belong and whom I serve stood beside me and said, "Do not be afraid, Paul. You must stand trial before Caesar; and God has graciously given you the lives of all who sail with you." So keep up your courage, men, for I have faith in God that it will happen just as he told me.* (Acts 27:23–25)

Who told Paul? God told him. And how did God tell him? He told Paul through a messenger. God assigned the angel to bring the revelation to Paul, to let him know they would all be okay. The ship would be lost, but all would survive the shipwreck. And it happened just as the angel had spoken. So, some angels are assigned to bring us revelation.

## ACTIVATING THE ANGELS: THE SIT PRINCIPLE

Each of us longs to make a spiritual connection that enables God's plans to be fully realized in us during our lifetime. God surrounds us with His angels as support-workers and helpers, to assist us in accomplishing our God-given destiny. Powerful things happen when you learn how to engage with the angelic realm.

Angels surround us, but you must put them to work. They are not waiting for your feelings or pain. They will not automatically respond to obstacles or difficulties. If that were the case, your choices wouldn't matter. But God honors your choice. He respects your decisions. He limits Himself to your faith only because He honors you. (See Deuteronomy 30:19; Joshua 24:15.) The Scriptures declare, *"Truly, I say to you, whatever you bind on earth shall be bound in heaven, and whatever you loose on earth shall be loosed in heaven"* (Matthew 18:18 ESV).

**THE S.I.T. PRINCIPLE**

**S**peak the Word  Psalm 103:20-21

**I**nterceed (Spend Time In Prayer)  Acts 10:2

**T**ouch God  (Through Your Giving)  Acts 10:4

Through my own personal encounters in the glory realm, I was given three keys that activate the angelic realm. I like to call this the *SIT Principle* because it's not something done in haste. We must take the time necessary to become familiar with the angelic realm as we encounter the glory. *"Be still, and know that I am God"* (Psalm 46:10).

## 1. SPEAK THE WORD

Psalm 103:20–21 (AMPC) says,

> *Bless (affectionately, gratefully praise) the Lord, you His angels, you mighty ones who do His commandments, hearkening to the voice of His word. Bless (affectionately, gratefully praise) the Lord, all you His hosts, you His ministers who do His pleasure.*

This Scripture gives us the understanding that angels move in obedience to the voice of God's word. His angels do His commands. The Scriptures call these angelic messengers *"ministers who do His pleasure."* What is the pleasure of God today? What are His commands today?

The commands of God for today are all found in His Word, but that Word must be given a voice because angels respond to the voice of God's word. When God's word is spoken, angels are assigned to go after that word and bring it into manifestation. I'm not talking about any kind of words; I'm talking about God's words. When we speak the words of God, angels go into action to fulfill what we speak.

How do you activate angels? And how do you know which angels to activate? Speak the Word of God, according to what you need. Find a promise in the Word of God, and use it boldly. He watches over His Word to perform it.

> UNDER THE OLD COVENANT, THE PEOPLE OF GOD DIDN'T HAVE AUTHORITY TO COMMAND ANGELS. TODAY ANGELS WAIT FOR US TO COMMAND THEM, BECAUSE WE HAVE BEEN GIVEN AUTHORITY OVER THEM IN THE NAME OF JESUS.

Under the old covenant, the people of God didn't have authority to command angels. Today angels wait for us to command them, because we have been given authority over them in the name of Jesus. Yes, as those in Christ, we now have authority over the angelic realm. (See 1 Peter 3:22.) The Scriptures even say that we will judge angels. (See 1 Corinthians 6:3.) You cannot judge something unless you have legal authority over it. So speak the Word, and watch your angels move into action.

If you make scriptural declarations about healing, healing angels will be released. If you make scriptural declarations about family, ministering angels will be released to touch your family.

As an example, the Scriptures declare, *"The LORD be magnified, who delights in the prosperity of His servant"* (Psalm 35:27 NASB). If God takes pleasure in the prosperity of His servants, how much more does He take pleasure in the prosperity of His children? We are not only servants; we are heirs, joint heirs with Christ in God. (See Romans 8:16–18.) God wants to bless us. If you're having financial difficulties or problems with provision of any kind, declare that word. Say:

> God, You take pleasure in my prosperity. You said it in Your Word. So, right now, Lord, I thank You that You are activating angels of prosperity in my life. They are being activated right now to respond to my needs, to any area where I am lacking sufficient supply. I thank You for releasing those angels, that are even now responding to the voice of Your Word. I invite Your angels to do their work, even as I invite Your Spirit to speak to me now. And I receive it. Amen!

This lays a foundation. You need to take it, make it your own, and live this thing out. Don't do it haphazardly, hit or miss, and don't just experience it once in a while. Do it on a regular basis. Keep building on your experience. In declaring the Word this way, we've activated angels. How? By stepping out in faith.

Will you feel those angels? Not necessarily. Will you see those angels? Not necessarily. But we know what the Word of God says, so we step out in faith on that Word. Remember, faith is always the beginning. When you step out in faith and begin to activate angels, speak the Scriptures and boldly declare them to come forth with the confidence of God. Eventually you will feel a shift in the atmosphere as your spiritual senses become aware that something is happening.

We have a resource available that can assist you in finding the right Scriptures to declare. It is called *The Word to Activate Angels*.[2] I encourage you to go online and begin using it right away. You must give voice to God's word through declaring His Word:

- Command angels to minister to your personal needs. (See Philippians 4:19.)

- Command angels to minister in your home. (See Joshua 24:15.)

- Command angels to minister to your family. (See Psalm 103:17.)

- Command angels to minister to your finances. (See 2 Corinthians 9:8.)

- Command angels to minister in your church. (See 2 Corinthians 3:6.)

## 2. INTERCEDE (SPEND TIME IN PRAYER)

Intercession becomes easy when you realize it's simply communication between you and God. Open up the airwaves between heaven and earth by having a dialogue with the Father. As you do this, angels are activated to move upon your prayers. As you move in the Spirit with your prayer language, this creates a supernatural tunnel in the Spirit for angels to quickly move into deep, strategic situations and accomplish God's purposes. Your prayers open the way for them:

> *Then he continued, "Do not be afraid, Daniel. Since the first day*
> *that you set your mind to gain understanding and to humble yourself*
> *before your God, your words were heard, and I have come in response*
> *to them."*                                        (Daniel 10:12)

This Scripture shows us that Daniel was able to release a chief angel through his prayers. The Lord clearly revealed this to me as one of the keys to engaging with the angelic realm.

The early church learned how to press into the Spirit through prayer to activate the angelic realm. (See Acts 12:5–11.) You can release angels through your prayers as well. This second realm of activation is connected to the second realm in the Spirit—the anointing. You must receive an anointing from the Holy Spirit to pray in this way. Not only do your prayers activate the angels to come and bring assistance, but your Spirit-led prayers will supernaturally open your eyes to see the reality of God's angels in your midst. This is a two-fold activation.

We need to remember the testimony of the Scriptures when Elisha seemed to be a threat to his enemy. The opposing forces gained momentum. The enemy armies and their chariots surrounded the city, and Elisha's servant became deeply worried. Elisha prayed for the servant's eyes to be opened to see the angelic presence. He wanted his servant to see the supernatural reality of victory that was taking place. (See 2 Kings 6:15–17.) It's vital that you begin seeing things in the Spirit. Your prayers make that necessary spiritual connection. The angels of God await your instructions, your words of command in prayer. (See Revelation 5:8.)

## 3. TOUCH GOD (THROUGH YOUR GIVING)

In this third step of activation, you must yield yourself in a new way to the realm of the heavenlies. Press into it. Respond to it. Angels are waiting for you. This third activation connects directly with the third realm in the Spirit, the glory.

We find an interesting testimony in Acts:

> *At Caesarea there was a man named Cornelius, a centurion in what*
> *was known as the Italian Regiment. He and all his family were devout*

*and God-fearing; he gave generously to those in need and prayed to*
*God regularly.*                                                        (Acts 10:1–2)

Cornelius was a devout, reverential man and devoted to the things
of God. He gave, and he prayed continually. Then something wonderful happened:

*One day at about three in the afternoon he had a vision. He dis-*
*tinctly saw an angel of God, who came to him and said, "Cornelius!"*
*Cornelius stared at him in fear. "What is it, Lord?" he asked. The*
*angel answered, "Your prayers and gifts to the poor have come up as*
*a memorial offering before God."*                          (Acts 10:3–4)

The angel specifically mentioned Cornelius's prayers and his gifts
to the poor. These two elements went up to God as a sacrifice and
caused Cornelius to be remembered.

What happens when you pray? What happens when you begin to
give to God, when you decide to no longer be stingy, when you give
yourself to the spirit of generosity? When you enter into the flow of
sowing into the heavens, purposing in your heart to give in the way
God desires, the way the Scriptures teach, your generosity rises before
God as a memorial, and heaven takes notice.

A memorial has someone's name engraved on it.
When you pray and sow your seed with purpose,
your name is suddenly on heaven's lips. When
God saw the memorial sent by Cornelius's
prayers and giving, He said, "Let's release
an angel to intervene for this man." That
was how it started. The end result was
an outpouring of glory in a household
full of Gentiles who were filled with the
Spirit and spoke in tongues.

> WHEN YOU ENTER
> INTO THE FLOW OF SOWING
> INTO THE HEAVENS, PURPOSING IN
> YOUR HEART TO GIVE IN THE WAY GOD
> DESIRES, THE WAY THE SCRIPTURES
> TEACH, YOUR GENEROSITY RISES
> BEFORE GOD AS A MEMORIAL, AND
> HEAVEN TAKES NOTICE.

If God did this for Cornelius and his
family, He will do it for you. While utilizing this third activation of the SIT Principle,
find a comfortable place where you can create an

atmosphere for the glory. Don't rush. Take time out of your busy schedule to engage with heaven in this way.

My wife, Janet, and I enjoy creating peaceful atmospheres in our home through the use of anointed instrumental music, scented candles, and low lighting. Don't think too much about seeing your angel at this point. It could hinder your experience. Instead, concentrate on the sweet presence of Jesus that surrounds you.

Ask God to speak to you concerning your financial stewardship. Ask Him to show you the spiritual fields where your seeds will produce the best harvest. Choose to live your life generously. Continually look for people, places, and atmospheres where you can sow the seeds of your life with the intention of cultivating an abundant harvest.

Touching God through your sacrificial giving of spirit, soul, and body is very personal, but extremely powerful. As you sow to the heavens, the Lord sows to the earth with a release of angelic helpers ready to assist and deliver blessings to you from the glory realm.

Dr. Roy Hicks offers this warning when it comes to working with your angels: "Your angel can be thwarted from lifting his hand to help you. Obey, obey, obey! Keep a smile on your Father's face as well as on the face of your angel. Work to keep your first love and stay as trusting as a child."[3] We discovered that a life of devoted obedience to the Spirit is a major factor in the active involvement of our angels. They will not and cannot operate against our free will, as free will is a gift God gave to all mankind. We must always choose obedience (see Joshua 24:15), and as we do, we liberate our angels to be actively involved in our lives.

When you obey these scriptural keys, you will have angelic impartation. Get in the glory cloud where angelic activity is imminent. Then bring others into that cloud too.

Are you hungry to go deeper in the Spirit? He has greater things prepared for you as you determine to enter into these *Glory Realms*.

# 6

# REALMS OF THE MIRACULOUS

*Very truly I tell you, whoever believes in me will do the works I
have been doing, and they will do even greater things than these,
because I am going to the Father.*
—John 14:12

The dictionary defines the word *miracle* as "an effect or extraordinary
event in the physical world that surpasses all known human or natural
powers and is ascribed to a supernatural cause." That makes it impossible to do this in the natural. A miracle is something only God can do.
The amazing thing is that He wants to release His miracles through
you and me.

## MIRACLE FOUNDATIONS IN FAITH

*So again I ask, does God give you his Spirit and work miracles among
you by the works of the law, or by your believing what you heard? So
also Abraham "believed God, and it was credited to him as righteousness." Understand, then, that those who have faith are children of
Abraham. Scripture foresaw that God would justify the Gentiles by
faith, and announced the gospel in advance to Abraham: "All nations
will be blessed through you." So those who rely on faith are blessed
along with Abraham, the man of faith.* (Galatians 3:5–9)

There are some requirements for being a modern-day miracle
worker. The first qualification for operating in creative miracles is that
you must have faith for miracles. That coincides with the first realm
in the spiritual dimension, the realm of faith. Faith comes by hearing
God's Word, and that Word becomes the power of God inside us.

The second qualification for operating in creative miracles is that you must be anointed with power. That coincides with the second realm in the Spirit, the realm of the anointing. It is impossible to work such miracles in our own strength. We need faith to believe that we have been anointed to work miracles in the name of Jesus Christ by the power of the Holy Spirit.

The third qualification for operating successfully in the miraculous is in yielding to God and flowing in His glory. More miracles happen in that realm, and they happen quickly.

## FAITH FOR HEALING

Progression into the realm of the miraculous begins with a solid foundation of faith. Jesus Christ saves, and He also heals. Romans 10:9 says, *"If you declare with your mouth, 'Jesus is Lord,' and believe in your heart that God raised him from the dead, you will be saved."* What are the steps to being saved? If you are reading this book, you may have already received salvation through Jesus Christ. If so, then you already know the steps to being saved. But if not, these are the steps you must take:

1. You hear the Word of God.

2. You believe the Word in your heart.

3. You confess faith in Christ unto salvation.

You hear, you believe, and you confess.

Interestingly, the steps to being healed are exactly the same, and healing is one of the dimensions God wants to unlock for you in this realm of the miraculous. When the Scriptures say, *"If you believe in your heart that God raised him from the dead, you will be saved,"* it does not just refer to spiritual salvation. The salvation God offers is for the spirit, the soul, and the body.[1] Being saved in your body refers to health and healing. So, for healing, you must follow the same three steps:

1. You hear the Word of God.

2. You believe the Word in your heart.

3. You confess or act in a way that confirms the healing.

The steps are the same, and the results are the same. First you believe, and then you receive, having complete confidence in God's Word to save you. (See James 1:21.) It is impossible to receive without first believing. If you want God to use you in the dimension of divine healing, start by finding out what God's Word says about healing. You can actually *medicate* on God's Word. Look at these Scriptures:

- Exodus 15:26

- Deuteronomy 5:33

- Psalm 30:2; 107:20

- Proverbs 3:1–2; 16:24

- Isaiah 53:4–5

- Jeremiah 17:14

- Matthew 4:23–24; 12:15

- Mark 3:10; 11:23–24

- Luke 4:40

- John 10:10; 15:7

Focus on these healing Scriptures, and speak them aloud. Remember, faith comes by hearing, not by thinking. Your faith for healing is voice-activated at the sound of God's healing Word being spoken by you.

The process is the same for every other miracle you need from God, whether it be a financial miracle, a divine intervention in the midst of a family situation, or anything else. It begins in the realm of faith. This is how we pull the invisible into the visible plane. Through faith, we put a demand on the supernatural and move it into our natural realm. Find what you need in the Word, believe God's Word in your heart, and take action toward it.

## GREAT LOVE PRODUCES GREAT MIRACLES

The late Frances Hunter, one of my mentors in healing, often said, "Looking for feelings instead of healings can rob you of what God wants to do through you."[2] Remember that God's love is the greatest power available to us. It is available at all times, whether we feel it or not. We cannot be moved by feelings. We must be moved by *fillings*. If we're filled with the Holy Spirit and anointed by Him, then that's enough.

> GREAT MIRACLES HAPPEN WHEN WE DEVELOP COMPASSION FOR THE SICK AND HURTING BECAUSE GOD'S LOVE FLOWS THROUGH US.

Great miracles happen when we develop compassion for the sick and hurting because God's love flows through us. When we pray out of genuine compassion, we don't pray for them in the natural, out of pity. Compassion means we actually feel their pain and recognize how very much God loves them and wants them to be healed. In sensing what heaven has in store for them, we release God's love upon them. When we operate in God's love, miracles happen. Believe that God wants to do it, and He will.

## WORKING MIRACLES IN THE ANOINTING

What does working miracles look like? Faith always takes action. The same faith that saved you brings you healing, but your faith must be confirmed by a specific action. Hebrews 11:6 says, *"Without faith it is impossible to please God, because anyone who comes to him must believe that he exists and that he rewards those who earnestly seek him."* We're not asking God to do anything new or unusual. This is key to understanding the dimension of the miraculous. The atmosphere of miracles is already available to us, just as electricity is always available to us. Instead of asking God to do something, we're simply thanking Him for what He has already done and tapping into what already exists. He is the Rewarder. We just receive His supernatural gift by cooperating with the Spirit.

The way God releases His healing through you varies according to the situation and the specific instruction you receive from heaven. This requires your willingness to flow in obedience with the anointing.

When we launch into miracle ministry, fully trusting God to work through us, we will get "God results." Let the supernatural become your natural. This may sound like an oxymoron, but God wants a flow of miraculous power to become a natural occurrence in our lives.

Since we are all different, what this flow looks like will also be different. Each of us has his or her own method. In whatever way God ministers through you, that's the right way. When you lay hands on the sick, you will have your own style, your own way of praying, your own form of speech, your own vocal inflections, and your own facial expressions. Do what is natural for you. Be natural in being supernatural. Let the power of God flow naturally through you. He created you to operate in this way.

## SUPERNATURAL METHODS FOR WORKING MIRACLES

Various styles and techniques are used when working miracles. Some will be new to you, things you've never read about or never seen done by anyone else. That's exciting because the Spirit wants to do new things through you! In the meantime, let's look at examples of people working miracles in the Scriptures.

You can lay hands on the sick. Mark 16:18 says, *"They will place their hands on sick people, and they will get well."* Mark 1:40–42 shows that Jesus healed a leper with a touch. In Mark 7, Jesus put His fingers into a deaf man's ears, and they opened. There is power in laying your hands on someone for their healing. When Jesus did it, the sick were healed. It will work for you too.

There are many different methods of laying hands on the sick. Let the Spirit lead you. You can place your hands on the person's head, on their neck, or on the affected area. You might be led to have the person put their hand on the area of need, and then you place your hands over their hands or on their head. There is no one right way. You are anointed to work miracles. God is faithful to show you how. Be willing to listen to His still small voice in the process.

When I minister to the sick, I ask God to show me how to lay hands on them. He often gives me specific instructions for doing it, depending upon the condition I'm dealing with. For instance, when praying for healing from carpal tunnel syndrome, I ask the person to stretch out the arm that bothers them. I begin working the miracle by commanding those muscles to strengthen and for the carpal tunnel area to open. Medically speaking, this issue causes pressure on the median nerve, resulting in subsequent weakness in the wrist. When approaching it spiritually, I deal with these issues one by one. I have had great success in ministering this way. Hundreds have been freed from their pain and given a new start.

Amanda, from Auckland, New Zealand, testified:

...from that day you prayed for me I have been healed. Completely! Praise the Lord! I was under the top hand special-ist here in Auckland, and that very week after I was healed I had two appointments scheduled—one with the neurologist at Auckland Hospital and the second an MRI scan at the largest hospital in New Zealand. Well, after both tests, the team of hand specialists have written a letter to my family doctor stat-ing that there are no longer any symptoms of carpal tunnel, and they have dismissed me from the government medical system. Hallelujah!

Once you witness a miracle and realize that God can do it through you, you will be able to do it everywhere you go.

Several years ago, I asked the Spirit for His strategy concerning ministry to the thyroid gland because so many people needed a mir-acle touch in this area. He directed me to minister specifically to the hypothalamus and pituitary gland since those are the central con-trol centers for the thyroid. Although the thyroid sits in the front of the neck, those control centers are located between the eyes and the temples. From that time on, whether praying for an overactive or an underactive thyroid, I position my hands on the sick person with my thumbs between their eyes and my four fingers on their temples, in front of the ears. The results have been wonderful because this instruc-tion was given to me by God for working this miracle.

God will give you His specific instructions too. His promise is that when you lay your anointed hands on the sick, they will recover. The power of God inside of you is greater than any other power that's in the world. His Word declares, *"The one who is in you is greater than the one who is in the world"* (1 John 4:4).

Don't be afraid of coming into contact with sickness. If you're filled with the Holy Spirit, you are anointed to work miracles. Every sickness must yield to the power of healing that flows through you.

Recognize that life-giving power flows through your hands. When you reach out to heal the sick, your hands become the portals for heaven to touch earth. Embrace that truth as you begin working miracles.

> WHEN YOU REACH OUT TO HEAL THE SICK, YOUR HANDS BECOME THE PORTALS FOR HEAVEN TO TOUCH EARTH. EMBRACE THAT TRUTH AS YOU BEGIN WORKING MIRACLES.

When ministering to the deaf, I've often stuck my fingers in their ears, commanded their hearing to be restored, and then witnessed the miracle happen before my eyes. When ministering to the blind, I've placed my fingers directly upon their eyes and commanded them to open with clarity of vision, and it happens just like that.

## DEMONSTRATION BRINGS MANIFESTATION

In my travels around the world, I've enjoyed observing the various ways that different ministers operate in their unique anointings with demonstrations as directed by the Spirit. Some ministers blow upon people as they impart the gifts of the Holy Spirit. (See John 20:22.) Others wave their hands or their suit jacket toward the crowd.

I've seen, and even done, some very radical things, but we have biblical precedence for these things:

- Moses stretched forth his rod to part the Red Sea. (See Exodus 14:16.)

- Elisha threw down his mantle to divide the waters of the Jordan River. (See 2 Kings 2:14.)

- Paul said, *"My message and my preaching were not with wise and persuasive words, but with a demonstration of the Spirit's power"* (1 Corinthians 2:4).

- Jesus made mud with His spit and put it into a blind man's eyes, and he recovered his sight. (See John 9:6–7.)

- Jesus cast demons out of a man everybody thought was crazy, sending them into a herd of pigs, and delivered him. (See Luke 8:26–33.)

- Jesus pulled money out of a fish's mouth in order to pay His taxes. (See Matthew 17:24–27.)

All these examples are biblical demonstrations for working miracles.

I once asked my friend LeRoy Jenkins, an old-time gospel tent preacher, what his number one key was for working miracles. He said, "I don't like to lose a fight. I'm determined to win!" If you know what God's Word says about miracles, you can have the confidence to work them in the anointing.

If you're ministering to someone in a wheelchair, and have the confidence of God that they will walk again, you need to do something about it. You can't just let them sit in that chair, receive your prayer, and go home the same way. You must work that miracle.

What should you do? Either you or those who work with you can pull that person up from the chair and give them an opportunity to step out in faith. If someone uses a walker, cane, or crutch, invite them to walk without them. They may take small steps in the beginning, but working the miracle is the only way the power of God will be seen when you lay hands on the sick. The manifestation comes through demonstration. Be sensitive in each case, following the leading of God's Spirit. You will be surprised at the results you receive.

Not only can you lay hands on the sick, but this also works in reverse. If the sick touch you, they can be instantly healed. There are quite a few biblical examples of this. (See Mark 5:25–34; Mark 6:56; Luke 6:19.) It works because the power in you is greater than the power of the sickness.

I've had people touch the edge of my jacket (their point of contact) while I've been ministering, and miraculous things took place. Heart conditions were healed, cancers disappeared, and tumors dissolved.

People can also be healed when you speak to the sickness and command it to leave (see Matthew 8:8; Mark 11:23), or through a Spirit-given word of knowledge. It's simple. God gives you a word about healing, and you speak it. When the person responds to that word, they are healed.

Healing can also come through anointing the sick with oil which represents the Holy Spirit. (See Mark 6:12–13; James 5:14–15.) I sometimes anoint people with the sign of the cross. At other times, I slather their heads with the oil, again, depending upon the leading of the Spirit.

Healing can come when people fall under the power of the Spirit. Healing can also come through the use of prayer clothes or anointed cloths, as we call them. (See Acts 19:11–12.) One thing is certain: the miracle comes when we put our faith into action. (See Luke 6:6–10; John 9:1–7.) In the anointing, we are given the responsibility to work the miracle.

## MOVING INTO MIRACLE-WORKING GLORY

Once you've established your faith in the miraculous, worked miracles in the anointing, and seen supernatural results, you must make room for the testimony. Testimonies are essential for building a greater cloud of glory and activating the greater glory corporately. When God's miracles are shared, victory is released in that testimony (see Revelation 12:11; 19:10), opening a realm for somebody else to experience the same dimension of God's goodness.

A shared testimony is prophetic in nature, pregnant with miracles, and can reproduce the same result in others. When we stand in the realms of glory, we declare God's miracles, and more miracles take place easily. In these moments, you don't need the laying on of hands or the anointing with oil. In the glory, God's cloud comes upon you and envelops you within the mist of His miracles. Often, this happens to many people at one time.

> WHEN GOD'S MIRACLES ARE SHARED, VICTORY IS RELEASED IN THAT TESTIMONY, OPENING A REALM FOR SOMEBODY ELSE TO EXPERIENCE THE SAME DIMENSION OF GOD'S GOODNESS.

It was the glory of God that hovered in the beginning of time, and it was in that glory God spoke all of creation into existence:

*Now the earth was formless and empty, darkness was over the surface of the deep, and the Spirit of God was hovering over the waters. And God said, "Let there be light," and there was light.* (Genesis 1:2–3)

When the glory comes, all you need to do is speak God's Word into the atmosphere, and the universe responds with divine alignment. Speaking a now word brings a now manifestation. Reach into the glory realm, receive the revelation of heaven in your spirit, and bring it forth with your voice.

This is different from working miracles in the anointing or establishing a realm for miracles by faith. In this dimension, we speak the revelation of heaven, and it becomes prophetic to our situation. Complete openness to the Spirit allows the glory of God to invade our lives through the sound of our voices. *"By faith we understand that the universe was formed at God's command, so that what is seen was not made out of what was visible"* (Hebrews 11:3).

As we speak, the miracle is released, but still must be grasped. When standing in the glory, ask the person in need to do something they could not do before. That helps them engage with the miracle that is being released.

This works for you too. For instance, if the Spirit gives you a word that backs are being healed and you've had pain in your back, move it. This is not to look for the pain, but to notice the miracle, to see what God has done.

We never look for pain or sickness in the glory. They can't be found in that realm. Looking for sickness and pain pulls you back into the realm of natural limitation. Notice the miracle instead.

We always tell people, "Check seven times." Why is that? Naaman was instructed to dip in the Jordan River seven times. Not until the seventh time did the miracle manifest. (See 2 Kings 5:1–14.) Just because you don't see anything the first time you check doesn't mean it hasn't happened. In the glory, it's already there. It's in the atmosphere. Check, and keep checking, until the miracle manifests. Then thank God for it. This is often the way people receive the supernatural miracle of instant weight loss. As they check their waistline, they notice the difference happening for them in the midst of the glory.

## RELEASING ANGELIC MINISTERS IN THE GLORY

As we minister in the glory cloud, angels are an integral part of that interaction, bringing supernatural substances from the invisible into the visible realms. And, as I have already noted, we must learn how to minister with the angels. An important aspect of the glory realm is the present-day ministry of angels. As you speak in the glory, your words release and activate angels to move on divine assignment.

When the Spirit first began teaching me about the importance of angelic ministry, I was on a month-long ministry trip to New Zealand. During one of the evening meetings at the Town Hall in Papatoetoe, when I spoke from the floor level, the curtains on the stage behind me swung back and forth. It was as if a wind had blown into the auditorium, forcefully moving the curtains to and fro. This was not a momentary event but continued on and on.

In the Scriptures, angels are referred to as *spirit winds.* (See Ezekiel 37:9; John 3:8; Acts 2:2.) *"You commandeered winds as messengers, appointed fire and flame as ambassadors"* (Psalm 104:4 MSG). *"Regarding angels he says, The messengers are winds, the servants are tongues of fire"* (Hebrews 1:7 MSG). I believe what happened that night was a sign of angelic ministry being made available to us in the glory realm. In those meetings, many wonderful healings and unusual miracles took place. God taught us about angels and how to interact with them.

One of the things I've learned is that the presence of angels must be recognized in order to be utilized. Of course, we don't worship the angels, but we must honor their presence when they come, by recognizing what they are doing. In a ministerial setting, this could be as simple as saying, "I welcome the ministering angels in this place tonight," or "I see miracle angels being released to minister to your need." In a personal encounter, you might say something like, "I see you, and I thank God you're here."

Moses had an encounter in which: *"The angel of the LORD appeared to him in a blazing fire from the midst of a bush.... So Moses said, 'I must turn aside now and see this marvelous sight'"* (Exodus 3:2–3 NASB). Notice that Moses recognized the angel and went out of his way to pay attention to the message being given to him through that angel. As you learn how to watch the atmosphere for the presence of angels, signs, and wonders, you will operate in a whole new level of the miraculous.

## SIGNS AND WONDERS IN THE GLORY

Moving in the dimension of signs and wonders requires a perceptive spirit and a willingness to flow in the spontaneity of the glory. We do not command signs and wonders to come forth as much as we watch for them to appear and recognize the movement of God within the glory realm. The dimension of glory overflows with signs that must be noticed.

> WE DO NOT COMMAND SIGNS AND WONDERS TO COME FORTH AS MUCH AS WE WATCH FOR THEM TO APPEAR AND RECOGNIZE THE MOVEMENT OF GOD WITHIN THE GLORY REALM.

The dictionary defines the word *sign* as "a token; indication; any object, action, event, pattern, etc. that conveys a meaning; a conventional or arbitrary mark figure, or symbol used as an abbreviation for the word or the words it represents; a notice, bearing a name, direction, warning, or advertisement that is displayed or posted for public view." These definitions help us understand signs and wonders and how to flow in them.

A sign is a token of God's love, a reminder that we are God's children. He really loves us! I have met many people around the world who told me when they experienced the glory realm, they felt the warm embrace of God's loving arms wrapped around them. The glory loves you.

Sometimes, the most significant signs come to us when we feel discouraged or helpless. God sends reminders that He will never leave us because He is eternally committed to our well-being.

## THE VOICE OF THE SIGN

*And it shall come to pass, if they will not believe thee, neither hearken to the voice of the first sign, that they will believe the voice of the latter sign.* (Exodus 4:8 KJV)

Signs convey a specific message while the Spirit speaks in the language of miracles. To ignore His signs is to ignore His voice. To deny His signs is to deny His Word. A sign is "a conventional or arbitrary mark using abbreviation for the word or words that it represents." Each sign has a voice and conveys a message, representing something God is saying or something He is doing. Therefore, when God pours out signs, we cannot be passive and think, *Oh, that's nice.* We must ask Him, "God, what is it that You are saying to me through this sign?"

The ultimate purpose of any sign is to make you wonder. When it is a holy sign from God, it always points you to the person and presence of Jesus Christ. While ministering in Hong Kong with Pastors Rob and Glenda Rufus, the supernatural oil poured so profusely from my hands that we collected it in a glass cup and used it to anoint hundreds of people who attended the Grace and Glory Conference.

This oil that flowed from my hands had the fragrance of vanilla. "What does vanilla signify?" I asked. One lady said that it represented intimacy. The Holy Spirit was speaking to us about intimacy, so we leaned into that revelation to hear further from heaven. There is a voice in each sign, and we must ask what God is saying to us.

On another occasion, I was ministering at a Mountaintop Encounter with Dr. A. L. and Joyce Gill in Big Bear Lake, California. When the supernatural oil flowed during my ministry, it smelled like cedar. While pondering this, the Lord took me to Psalm 92. Verse 10 says, *"You have exalted my horn like that of a wild ox; fine oils have been poured on me."*

Verses 12–15 say,

*The righteous will flourish like a palm tree, they will grow like a cedar of Lebanon; planted in the house of the LORD, they will flourish in the courts of our God. They will still bear fruit in old age, they will stay fresh and green, proclaiming, "The LORD is upright; he is my Rock, and there is no wickedness in him."*

This Scripture speaks about the strength and prosperity of God that comes as we are *"planted in the house of the Lord."* Because the oil was dripping from my hands, I asked everybody in attendance to form a circle around the inside of the conference room so I could release this impartation. As I laid my hands upon the people, they fell out in the Spirit. When I laid my hands on one young lady who suffered from scoliosis of the spine, her back straightened and she was completely healed. Many more healings took place that morning along with extraordinary manifestations, including the piano playing on its own and angels singing over us. We stood in awe at the glory of the Lord.

Not long after, I was at a conference in Saskatoon, Saskatchewan, with my dear friend and healing evangelist Joan Hunter. The oil flowed with the fragrance of cedar again. Clearly, the Spirit was trying to communicate a specific message to us. I shared Psalm 92 with Joan, and when she read it in her Bible, her translation rendered the latter part of verse 14 as, *"They are ever full of sap and green"* (ESV).

In the cedar-scented oil, Joan felt the Lord was saying that He was pouring out His sap through us. I asked her, "What is that sap?" She said, "It's supernatural anointing and prosperity—SAP." That became our theme for the rest of the conference, and many miracles occurred. We must listen to the voice of the sign.

## RECOGNIZING THE SIGNS

Open your eyes to see God in His glory. Jesus prayed this would happen:

> *Father, I want those you have given me to be with me where I am, and to see my glory, the glory you have given me because you loved me before the creation of the world.* (John 17:24)

I've noticed that signs don't necessarily come to those who search for them, but appear unannounced around us daily. They must be noticed.

Signs follow our lives. There is a difference between searching for them and recognizing them, although the distinction may be subtle. If you look for signs, you will have difficulty finding them and may become frustrated. Your preconceived ideas about how God should appear can sometimes keep you blinded.

As believers, we are not to be like the Pharisees. We don't need signs in order to believe. (See Matthew 12:38–39.) We trust God and His purposes fully, regardless of what we see. We believe His Word, and we believe His Spirit. Our eyes are directed heavenward, and as we look unto Him, we recognize the glory of His presence. With our eyes are focused in this way, we notice His glory all around us. And when we see one sign, it leads to seeing more. One of the signs we see repeatedly in our ministry is that of the golden glory.

A minister named Peter came to my meetings in Kangirsuk, Nunavik. He was a respected elder in the community and carried a great anointing upon his life. During those meetings, he saw the golden glory that came and covered me during times of worship, but never became enamored with the sign. Instead, Peter fell in love with God's glory and walked in the glory everywhere he went. The glory was all he could think about, all he could talk about. The result of his eyes being fixed on the glory was his movement into a new dimension of signs and wonders.

Peter shared with me through a translator that at times, when having a meal with others, the glory would fall upon him to such a degree that the manifestation of golden glory gathered on their plates and in their tea cups. Others told me that he left golden footprints wherever he walked. Peter's life became a testimony of God's glory. He utilized these signs to win souls to Christ and minister healing on many occasions.

> AS WE FIX OUR EYES ON THE GLORY REALM, WE SEE THE SIGNS THAT GOD GIVES US. THE SIGNS, HOWEVER, ARE NOT THE FOCUS. THE GLORY OF GOD IS ALWAYS OUR MAIN FOCUS.

As we fix our eyes on the glory realm, we see the signs that God gives us. The signs, however, are not the focus. The glory of God is always our main focus.

There are times when I preach and notice a shimmering in the palm of my hands or the golden glory appear on the sleeves of my jacket. When I see this, I recognize what God is doing, become sensitive to the way He is moving, and invite others present to notice the signs too.

Another time, as I ministered in Orlando, Florida, my hands, face, and body shimmered with the golden glory. When I asked others in the congregation to look for this manifestation upon themselves, a number of them found they had the same manifestation happening to them.

I never get tired of experiencing God's miracles and signs. If I get even one tiny speck of golden glory on my hands, I'm thankful. If all you get is one piece, praise God for that one, and He'll multiply it into two. I think this manifestation is beautiful. Those who have experienced it can testify to the special glory this sign brings.

## THE DIFFERENCE BETWEEN SIGNS AND WONDERS

A *wonder* is defined as "something strange and surprising; a cause of surprise, astonishment, or admiration." It is also "a miraculous deed or event, a remarkable phenomenon." The Bible speaks of wonders taking place in the heavens and signs on the earth below. (See Acts 2:19.) God will do signs in us and through us, for we are of the earth. Signs will come upon us and flow out of us.

People often ask me, "Why do the signs come out of you? Why does the oil come out of your hands?" If the Holy Spirit resides in me and wants to come out, it follows that He will come out of me. Sometimes the revelation of God is so simple that we overlook it.

Every occurrence of the word *wonders* in the Bible is accompanied by the word *signs*. It's always *signs and wonders*. The two go together. Signs and wonders happen in the earth and also in the heavens. The *Holman Bible Dictionary* says, "A sign appeals to the understanding, whereas a wonder appeals to the imagination."[3] A wonder always causes people to marvel at the greatness of God. We saw such a wonder while in the small Arctic community of Kuujjuaq. I was originally scheduled to just pass through on my way home from Salluit, where I had ministered at their annual Gospel Music Festival. While there, the glory manifested in a powerful way.

Paul Lepage, from Kuujjuaq, was deeply touched by the presence of the Lord. He had never seen the glory tangibly appear in this way. One night, he asked, "Would you be willing to stay a few more days and do a home meeting in my community?" I agreed. Paul and his wife, Eva, gathered about ten believers in their home. Since I came on such short notice, it didn't allow time for any advertisement of the meetings. We trusted God to bring additional people.

On the first night, the glory cloud came into the meeting. A white haze covered the ceiling area. People received physical healings. One couple in attendance were covered with golden glory as God spoke personally to them.

The next night, an even more amazing thing happened. People who had not heard about the meetings showed up at the house where we were gathered. We asked, "How did you find out about this meeting?" They answered, "Because the northern lights are over this house, the most beautiful northern lights we've ever seen." People were responding to this wonder in the heavens.

I had seen the northern lights before. Usually they were a beautiful green that danced across the sky. But these lights were not just green. They were blue and pink, yellow and orange, and dancing directly above that house on a hill, at the end of the road.

Remember how the wise men followed the star? That's what this was like. As the people of that community responded to the wonder in the heavens, it led them right into that house. They heard the praise and worship. It was where God did miracles for them.

One woman who came needed a double-hip replacement and was scheduled for surgery the next day in Montreal. She had come to Kuujjuaq from her village and was to travel to the hospital by airplane the next day. She was touched by the glory cloud and her hips healed. She did go to Montreal the next day as planned. The doctors took more X-rays, then asked, "Why are you here?" The surgery was cancelled.

God's wonders are marvelous, and He receives all the glory. May the wonders of God fill your life as you encounter His glory in a greater way.

## WHAT SHOULD WE EXPECT?

What are some of the signs and wonders we should all expect in our lives and ministries? Here are a few of the most common ones.

- Casting out demons, speaking in new tongues, healing the sick (see Mark 16:17–18)
- Raising the dead and cleansing those who are diseased. (see Matthew 10:8)

- Holy laughter (see Proverbs 17:22; Psalm 2:4; 126:2; Job 8:21)

- Being drunk on new wine (see Acts 2:15; 2 Corinthians 5:13)

- Trembling and vibrating in the Spirit (see Exodus 19:16; Daniel 10:10; Isaiah 6:4; Acts 4:31)

- Falling under the power of God (see Ezekiel 1:28; Matthew 17:6; Acts 9:4; Revelation 1:17)

- Being caught up in trances and visions (see Acts 10:10; 22:17)

- Remaining speechless and filled with awe (see Daniel 10:15; Luke 1:22)

- Experiencing extraordinary manifestations of golden glory (see Exodus 34:30)

There is a lifting we sense as we go higher into these glory realms. Heaven is the limit, yet in the heavens there are no limitations. We have tasted water turned into heavenly wine and manna that materialized from the glory realm. Allow the Spirit to use you to bring forth the greater manifestations of heaven on earth. Sense the glory, see the glory, speak from the glory, and manifest this glory.

In our meetings, we've experienced raindrops falling, fresh dew appearing, glory clouds, flashes of blue lightning, angelic majesties with radiant light, rainbows appearing in unusual ways and unusual places (including complete darkness), and fragrant oil, wine, and honey flowing from our hands and feet with the aroma of heaven. All of these things are common in the realm of the Spirit. Some people feel the burning of God. Others feel the wind of the Spirit as it blows gently through their lives.

I spoke at a church in Ohio where the manifestation of a waterline encircled the walls of the sanctuary, about fifteen feet above the floor. This was a visible indication of the Spirit river having risen in that place. We need to go deeper, even as He is calling us higher.

In many instances, supernatural oil has dripped down the walls of church sanctuaries and homes. Prophetically speaking, the Spirit desires to fill His temple with power and glory. What we have seen in the past is only the beginning. We must keep moving in the glory. The Spirit is leading us to places where we will witness creative miracles of all kinds. The wheels turn and realms interact with each other, inviting us to learn how to manifest the realities of heaven's abundance in our lives. Step further into these glory realms, for there is so much more.

Are you hungry to go deeper in the Spirit? He has greater things prepared for you as you determine to enter into these *Glory Realms*.

# PART III
# MOVING IN THE HEAVENLIES

*The heavens were opened and I saw visions of God.*
—Ezekiel 1:1

# 7

# REALMS OF MANIFESTING WEALTH

*And my God will meet all your needs according to*
*the riches of his glory in Christ Jesus.*
—Philippians 4:19

The glory holds many riches. If you've never realized it, take a moment, and think about heaven.

Heaven is an extravagant place with pearl gates, gold-paved streets, and so many mansions it would be impossible to count them all. God is not poor, and His heavenly economy is not suffering from decline. He makes this bold statement within the Scriptures: *"The silver is mine, and the gold is mine"* (Haggai 2:8). Although we understand that true riches are those that are incorruptible, we must also believe the truth that God desires for His people to have the ability and capacity to fully function in their calling while here on the earth.

It's true that we can't take money with us to heaven. We won't need it there anyway. (See Matthew 6:19–21.) But we need money from heaven now in order to do what we're called to do here on the earth.

Money is a powerful supernatural tool when placed in the proper hands. More than ever before, I believe the Spirit wants to teach us how to access the riches of glory, how to pull down and manifest wealth from the heavenly realm.

## THE THREE DIMENSIONS OF MANIFESTING WEALTH

The Scriptures have a lot to say about this. Like the others, this sphere opens through three distinct dimensions: blessing, favor, and increase, which are connected to the three realms in the Spirit we've already discussed.

## BLESSING: THE COVENANT CONNECTOR

*Honor the LORD with your wealth, with the firstfruits of all your crops; then your barns will be filled to overflowing, and your vats will brim over with new wine.* (Proverbs 3:9–10)

God's blessings are mentioned more than six hundred times in the Scriptures.[1] There is no doubt about the truth that He really wants to bless you. In fact, the covenant He's made with you through His blood sacrifice is a covenant of blessing. The enemy has tried to connect you to generational bondages and curses (see John 10:10), but the blood of Jesus opened the way for you to be eternally connected to generational blessing (see Galatians 3:13–14; Genesis 24:1).

However, we make a daily choice to live in that blessing. Like any other spiritual reality, it must be pursued and obtained fully by faith: *"This day I call the heavens and the earth as witnesses against you that I have set before you life and death, blessings and curses. Now choose life, so that you and your children may live"* (Deuteronomy 30:19).

When we speak about faith in the area of finances, we begin by addressing the issue of tithing. While true that in the past the concept of tithing was abused to manipulate and control people, we cannot dismiss tithing altogether. It is a legitimate spiritual principle that was put into motion even before Moses and the Law. Abraham tithed to King Melchizedek four hundred years before the old covenant was ever put into place. (See Genesis 14:20; Hebrews 7:12.)

We don't tithe to break a curse. That was broken by the finished work of Jesus Christ at the cross.[2] We tithe to break agreement with the spirit of fear over our finances.

The tithe was established at 10 percent, which is what the word *tithe* actually means. When we speak about tithing, we're talking about giving away 10 percent of our finances. For some people, this is a huge step. Generosity is a major theme throughout the Scriptures, and we know that God Himself is generous in every way. (See Proverbs 19:17; Matthew 10:42; John 3:16.) Unfortunately, the practice of generosity hasn't always prevailed within society. Fear of lack and uncertainties about the future have prevented some from being generous. This must change if we truly want to connect to the blessing dimension.

FEAR OF LACK AND UNCERTAINTIES ABOUT THE FUTURE HAVE PREVENTED SOME FROM BEING GENEROUS. THIS MUST CHANGE IF WE TRULY WANT TO CONNECT TO THE BLESSING DIMENSION.

A suffocating spirit of fear attempts to prevent God's people from being generous. The reality is that wherever fear is present, faith is absent. A practical way to break through the atmosphere of fear is to connect with the covenant blessing by determining to tithe, knowing that your faith is in God, not your money.

That's why the tithe is so powerful. It is a statement of faith, a declaration of praise, an announcement to God, "You are Jehovah Jireh! You are my Provider!" Tithing becomes a line drawn in the sand for your financial future, a line that boldly states, "I will not allow my finances to rule over me. I will rule over my finances."

In the business arena, we can look down through history and discover that the most successful people have been those with a desire to be generous. Modern-day multibillionaire Warren Buffet, known as one of the most successful investors of all time, has already donated 35 percent of his income to charity, and has pledged to donate as much as 85 percent of his estate within his lifetime.[3] That is much more than a tithe.

## A TALE OF TWO BROTHERS

In the Scriptures, we read the testimony of Jacob and Esau. (See Genesis 25:29–34.) It's an interesting story about satisfying an immediate desire and the willingness to let go of something precious in the heat of the moment. The end result was that Esau sold Jacob his birthright for a bowl of soup. Can you imagine selling your inheritance for such a small and menial thing? What a terrible trade that was!

Sure, Esau was hungry, but surely there was something he could have done besides selling his birthright. That birthright would have guaranteed him special authority within the family (he was next in line to his parents), a double-portion of inheritance, the Father's blessing, and the inheritance of the land of Canaan. I don't care how good a clam chowder tastes. It's not worth the price of a birthright.

You know what amazes me though? I have met so many wonderful people who love the Lord, yet have not discovered the joy of honoring the Lord with their finances. Many of them have a problem with the system of tithing, considering it to have been just an old covenant regulation under the Law. They feel that they should be able to decide what they want to give and when they want to give it. The problem with this thinking is that it's contrary to the Scriptures.

Jesus encouraged tithing. (See Matthew 23:23; Luke 11:42.) Generosity must become a lifestyle decision. Just like Esau made a terrible trade for his birthright, many people sell the blessing of God on their lives because they are unwilling to be generous. Our tithe is where our generosity begins. If we have a problem giving the tithe, how will we react when the Spirit asks for our all?

One of the ways to begin walking in the blessing of God is by becoming a blessing to others. When our focus shifts from our own needs to helping meet the needs of those around us, that's when the real miracle happens. Fear is removed from the equation because we are no longer self-focused but now guided by the spirit of generosity.

The tithe enables us to walk in a special level of faith that connects us to the blessing dimension. And there's still a lot more that the Spirit wants to give you.

## FAVOR: DIVINE ASSIGNMENT AND DIVINE ALIGNMENT

*Let love and faithfulness never leave you; bind them around your neck, write them on the tablet of your heart. Then you will win favor and a good name in the sight of God and man.* (Proverbs 3:3–4)

I discovered an amazing connection between our faithfulness to obey the leading of the Spirit and the divine favor of God. Since we are addressing the issue of manifesting wealth, I must mention that our faithfulness to hear the Spirit's voice regarding finances is critical. The connection between our offerings and favor works in the same way as the connection between the tithe and blessing. I am not saying you can buy favor; you can't do that. However, throughout the Scriptures, people positioned their lives to receive generously from the Spirit as they aligned their hearts with the heart of God.

We serve a generous God, and He wants us to connect with that reality. I have met many people around the world who struggle every day in the area of finances. They refuse to tithe and refuse to give financial offerings. Each of them is completely loved by God (there is no question about that), and He has already made every blessing available to them. But the question remains: Why are they not prospering? Do they have information about God's favor? Do they have a revelation about His desire to bless their life?

Information is useless without a revelation. Information can cause you to know about favor and yet still lack results. But a revelation will cause you to move toward an activation in order to produce a manifestation of the impartation. God's revelation will always motivate you toward generosity.

> INFORMATION IS USELESS WITHOUT A REVELATION. INFORMATION CAN CAUSE YOU TO KNOW ABOUT FAVOR AND YET STILL LACK RESULTS. BUT A REVELATION WILL CAUSE YOU TO MOVE TOWARD AN ACTIVATION IN ORDER TO PRODUCE A MANIFESTATION OF THE IMPARTATION.

In the Old Testament, King David delighted to see his people give willingly to the Lord. (See 1 Chronicles 29:9.) How much more, as new covenant believers, should we seek to freely give to Him? God is able to give you a special grace (or anointing) for giving. Ask Him for it. As Paul wrote, *"But since you excel in everything—in faith, in speech, in knowledge, in complete earnestness and in the love we have kindled in you—see that you also excel in this grace of giving"* (2 Corinthians 8:7).

## THE DIFFERENCE BETWEEN AN OFFERING AND THE TITHE

How is an offering different from the tithe? An offering is something the Spirit requests and to which we respond. Offerings come in all shapes and sizes. It's not a set percentage like the tithe. Sometimes, offerings are small, and at other times, they are huge. The key is that the Spirit sets the amount of the offering in answer to our prayer. We ask, "God, what would you have me give to this person, place, or situation?" then we wait to hear the response from His still, small voice that speaks with such inward clarity. Such prayers lead us to the Spirit's favor and divine connection.

I know many people who live this lifestyle of generosity. They tithe regularly, but also take time in their prayer life to ask God where and how they might be a blessing to others. Recently, we received a special gift in the mail from our friend, Tracey. One of the most generous people we know, she constantly looks for people and places where she can be a blessing in spirit, soul, and practical ways. She lives a generous lifestyle, and in return, we've noticed that she is extremely blessed.

Tracy also has favor on her life. The Spirit opens doors and opportunities for her that others might not have because she has positioned her life in a way that is open to both give and receive.

## THE SPIRIT REQUESTS THE OFFERING

Consider the story of Cain and Abel:

*Now Abel kept flocks, and Cain worked the soil. In the course of time Cain brought some of the fruits of the soil as an offering to the Lord. And Abel also brought an offering—fat portions from some of the firstborn of his flock. The Lord looked with favor on Abel and his offering, but on Cain and his offering he did not look with favor. So Cain was very angry, and his face was downcast. Then the Lord said to Cain, "Why are you angry? Why is your face downcast? If you do what is right, will you not be accepted? But if you do not do what is right, sin is crouching at your door; it desires to have you, but you must rule over it.* (Genesis 4:2–6)

Both Cain and Abel presented their offerings to God. But the Scriptures tell us that God refused Cain's offering while looking with favor on Abel and his offering. Why did this happen? God rejected Cain's offering because it was given in self-will and unbelief. Offerings must always be given in faith and obedience: *"By faith Abel brought God a better offering than Cain did. By faith he was commended as righteous, when God spoke well of his offerings"* (Hebrews 11:4.)

How does faith come? How do we present an offering to God in faith? Faith comes by hearing God's Word. (See Romans 10:17.) This is why it's so important to hear the voice of the Spirit about the offerings you give. The Spirit always sets the offering amount. He speaks, we hear, and we give our offerings in faith. We must listen to the revelation and be obedient to it. (See James 1:22.) This was what the early believers did:

> All the believers were one in heart and mind. No one claimed that any of their possessions was their own, but they shared everything they had. With great power the apostles continued to testify to the resurrection of the Lord Jesus. And God's grace was so powerfully at work in them all that there were no needy persons among them. For from time to time those who owned lands or houses sold them, brought the money from the sales and put it at the apostles' feet, and it was distributed to anyone who had need. (Acts 4:32–35)

Because all the believers were *"one in heart and mind,"* the new covenant church in Acts was given specific instructions from the Spirit about giving. The precedent was to give everything to the work of the gospel. They did this by putting everything they had into these offerings, selling lands, homes, and other valuables in order to lay the proceeds at the apostles' feet. And they did it with gladness and a spirit of generosity.

If we read farther into the book of Acts, however, we discover a couple in this community who did not obey the divine instructions that were given for the offering. Ananias and Sapphira lied about their offering, kept a portion for themselves, and gave only what remained. (See Acts 5:1–11.) The outcome for them was not favorable, to say the least, because what they did was in defiance of the Spirit's instruction.

## FINANCES FOR THE NATIONS

In the early days of my ministry, the Spirit spoke to me about going to Brazil. A few weeks after that desire was placed on my heart, I received a phone call from a pastor in Belo Horizonte, inviting me to come and minister to his church. It has always happened this way for us. The Lord gives us a burden for a specific nation, we lay hands on the map, sing and pray over that nation, and thank the Lord for opening the door. Within a short time, we generally receive a super-natural connection to go and minister there.

This pastor and I set the dates for spring of the following year. I asked him to call in a few months, confirming the arrangements for the venue and ministry details.

In the months that followed, I attempted to communicate by phone and email with that pastor, but I didn't hear from him until two weeks before the meetings were to begin. Because we hadn't heard anything, I assumed other plans had been made and that he no longer wanted me to come. I was so wrong!

When the pastor finally called, he told me about the advertising he had done, the churches he had lined up to cooperate, and the great time we were going to have when I came to minister in Belo Horizonte. Well, praise God, all of this was wonderful, except for the fact that it was only two weeks before departure, and I didn't have money for an airline ticket to Brazil.

I called my travel agent and asked her to find me the cheapest air-fare to Brazil. She called back and said it would be twenty-five hun-dred dollars. Where was I going to get that kind of money in the next few days? Janet and I went to prayer about it, and the Lord gave us a peace. A few days later, we filed our yearly income taxes and learned we would receive a tax refund of just over twenty-five hundred dol-lars. Hallelujah! Even though we needed that money to pay other bills, we committed it entirely to the Spirit, sensing that this was what He was asking of us as an offering.

The next week, as Janet took me to the airport for this trip, our son Lincoln cried in the back seat (he was just a baby at the time). Janet cried as she drove because I was leaving for two weeks, and she didn't have any money to pay the bills. Suddenly, a spirit of faith rose up in me. I knew God would not call me to the nations and leave my family deso-late as I traveled. We had presented our tithes and given our offerings in obedience to the Spirit, so we had a promise from the Scriptures. And I was determined to hold on to that promise for dear life.

That morning, we'd had some bills that needed to be paid and other financial matters that needed to be addressed for the ministry.

As a result, I had no spending money to take with me on the trip. Still, we knew that the Spirit had directed me to go to Brazil. When you have favor on your life, you don't have to worry about how it will all work out. You just do your part, and allow God to do His.

As we continued the drive to the airport, no money in our hands or in our bank accounts, we prayed. I asked Janet, "How much money do you need to pay the bills while I'm gone?"

She said, "We need a thousand dollars."

"Okay," I answered, "let's just trust God together that He will give us the thousand dollars that we need. I don't know how it will come to us, but we have the Lord's favor on our lives, so I know it will come."

We finished our prayer, and Janet dropped me off for my two-week trip to Brazil. At the same time my plane departed, Janet went to the mailbox and found a letter with a check for one thousand dollars in it. It was exactly what we needed and came from someone who had never given to our ministry before and never gave again. Even before we prayed, God had set the answer into motion.

I believe that our offerings had prepared the groundwork for a divine intervention of favor. The Lord had spoken to that person about sending us that exact amount of money. As he obeyed the Spirit, he became a catalyst for the miracle. Your offerings connect you with supernatural favor. That thousand-dollar provision came from an unusual and unexpected place, but this is what favor does for you. Generous offerings position you for generous favor. We have discovered that this principle of giving always works.

## INCREASE: THE POWER OF THE SEED

*Now he who supplies seed to the sower and bread for food will also supply and increase your store of seed and will enlarge the harvest of your righteousness. You will be enriched in every way so that you can be generous on every occasion, and through us your generosity will result in thanksgiving to God.* (2 Corinthians 9:10–11)

We have explored the two foundational dimensions of blessing and favor. Opening the third dimension has the ability to take you farther than you've ever been before. This is the dimension of expo-nential increase, the dimension of the seed.

Seed is always planted for a harvest. In 2 Corinthians 9:7, God's Word declares, *"Each of you should give what you have decided in your heart to give, not reluctantly or under compulsion, for God loves a cheer-ful giver."* So we understand that the seed is set according to our own desires, what we decide in our own heart to give. This is different from tithing and giving offerings.

Within the Scriptures, the concept of *seed* is sometimes referred to as *alms*, but they are the same. A seed is something we hold in our hand and know is not our harvest. The Spirit gives us the choice to either sow the seed or keep it. But we receive increase in this dimension according to the seed sown, depending on what we have purposed in our heart to do.

> THE SPIRIT GIVES US THE CHOICE TO EITHER SOW THE SEED OR KEEP IT. BUT WE RECEIVE INCREASE IN THIS DIMENSION ACCORDING TO THE SEED SOWN, DEPENDING ON WHAT WE HAVE PURPOSED IN OUR HEART TO DO.

This means the possibilities for our seed are unlimited. In other words, there is no limit to the supernatural har-vest you can receive in this dimension. Amazing! If we sow a generous seed, we can expect the Spirit to bring us a gener-ous harvest. The degree to which we sow will be the same degree to which we will reap. As Ruth Ward Heflin said, "As we sow to the heavens, He sows to the earth."[4] Our seed going up becomes a harvest coming down.

After we sow our seed, we should not look for a repayment from man. Our seed is not a loan or a favor given in anticipation of a favor to be received. The Scriptures make it clear that as we sow our seed, it is God who supernaturally repays: *"Whoever is kind to the poor lends to the LORD, and he will reward them for what they have done"* (Proverbs 19:17). In other words, it is God who brings the harvest.

We see this clearly displayed in nature. A farmer is responsible for going into his fields with seed to sow. It is God's job to cause fruit and vegetables to rise from the ground, to grow from that seed. Of course, the farmer must also tend to his crop as best as he can, but ultimately it is God who causes the harvest to come forth. This is the miracle of the seed. We sow, and God multiplies it back to us. He never adds. He always multiplies.

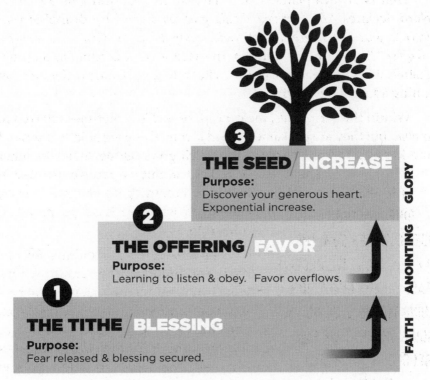

**THE SEED**/INCREASE
**Purpose:**
Discover your generous heart.
Exponential increase.

**THE OFFERING**/FAVOR
**Purpose:**
Learning to listen & obey. Favor overflows.

**THE TITHE**/BLESSING
**Purpose:**
Fear released & blessing secured.

GLORY

ANOINTING

FAITH

## MIRACLE MULTIPLICATION

*"How many loaves do you have?" he asked. "Go and see." When they found out, they said, "Five—and two fish." Then Jesus directed them to have all the people sit down in groups on the green grass. So they sat down in groups of hundreds and fifties. Taking the five loaves and the two fish and looking up to heaven, he gave thanks and broke the loaves. Then he gave them to his disciples to distribute to the people. He also divided the two fish among them all. They all ate and were satisfied, and the disciples picked up twelve basketfuls of broken pieces of bread and fish. The number of the men who had eaten was five thousand.* (Mark 6:38–44)

In biblical times, a loaf of bread was not very large. The largest ones were about five or six inches in diameter and about an inch thick (about the size of three slices of our modern-day bread), but more solid. One man could easily eat an entire loaf, and some could eat several loaves. To feed five thousand men, plus women and children, Jesus must have multiplied those five loaves into five thousand or even twenty thousand loaves.

Jesus also multiplied two fish to as much as the crowd could eat and still have twelve baskets left over. This creative miracle of increase demonstrates that creation by the Spirit is possible.[5]

Elisha, by the gift of miracles, multiplied bread from twenty loaves to feed a hundred men. (See 2 Kings 4:42–44.) He did this as an ordinary man. God wants to manifest this same glory through you and me.

Every farmer understands that the more seed he plants, the more potential he has for increase. A successful farmer always plants seed in several fields. He knows if his seed doesn't produce successfully in one field, then surely it will bring increase in another, more fertile, one. (See Amos 9:13; John 4:35–38.)

The verb *sow* means "to plant seed for growth, especially by scattering." It also means "to set something in motion." When we sow our financial seeds into the glory, we bring ourselves into divine alignment with the Spirit and set ourselves in motion for increase. Through this simple act, we move into the Spirit's dimension for increase.

The farthest distance between you and your harvest is simply your seed. Your seed moves you closer to your future.

When a farmer plans for his coming harvest, he makes sure to plant more than enough seed. He doesn't say, "I want a hundred bean plants, so I guess I'll just plant a hundred bean seeds." When he sows with a harvest in mind, he scatters his seeds in great abundance. A farmer can never be sure which seed will grow into a harvest and which will fail to produce a crop. This is why we must scatter our seed widely when unlocking this realm of increase. We know the harvest is coming, but never know which of our financial seeds might bring forth the greatest return.

## MIRACLE MONEY APPEARING

When Janet and I were first married and living in San Diego, California, we lived on a very limited budget. I remember one week when we had only fifteen dollars left to our name. With that, we needed to put food on the table, pay the electric bill and the phone bill, and put gas in the car. We had to drive to church three times a week to minister, and it was a thirty-minute drive each way. We didn't know what we were going to do. We often counted our pennies, but just when we thought we were not going to make it, God supplied for us in a most unusual way.

One night at church, we were praising the Lord. A wonderful peace came over me. We decided to sow everything we had in the offering, trusting God for our needs. We had to trust Him, as there was no other way to make ends meet. At the end of the meeting, my friend Paul asked if I had any spare change for a soda. He needed just a few more cents. I didn't think I had anything to give him, but out of instinct, I reached into my pocket to look for loose coins. To my surprise, I felt something like paper money. Startled to think I might have another dollar left to my name, I pulled the money from my pocket and looked at it.

It was not a dollar bill. It was a one-hundred-dollar bill. I was dumbfounded. How did one hundred dollars get into my pocket? There was no normal explanation for this. Janet and I rejoiced, knowing this miracle was directly from heaven. We knew the Spirit had supernaturally placed that money in my pocket. As we were faithful to do our part, He was faithful to do His.

One hundred dollars wasn't everything we needed, but a good beginning. Learning how to celebrate the small miracles and the little victories position you for more.

Several years later, we witnessed this same kind of miracle for the multiplication of money while hosting our first conference in Canada. Janet and I raised our nightly offerings to the Lord and asked Him to multiply them for the work of the ministry. We had heard the story of how Ruth Heflin's mother, Rev. Edith Heflin, once counted and recounted the offering after a revival meeting. As she persisted in prayer for the Lord to increase the finances, she experienced a multiplication of the offering until all the ministry bills could be paid. We knew if the Spirit could do this miracle for the Heflins, He could do it for us too.

After praying over the offerings, Janet and I counted them a second time. Sure enough, the money multiplied as our faith contended for this dimension of financial increase. In amazement, we counted the offerings again, making sure we had counted correctly. Each time we counted, we had a larger total. After tallying the offerings four times, the money settled at an amount that enabled us to pay all of our conference expenses. We praised the Lord. He is our supernatural Provider!

When you experience miracles like this in your finances, it causes faith to arise within you. Then, as you share your testimony, it releases an expectation into the atmosphere for those miracles to happen again. The Spirit teaches us how to manifest divine wealth, moving the riches of glory from heaven to earth.

At one of our summer camp meetings, I spoke about financial stewardship. The realms of glory opened with the possibility for money multiplication again. Many people got out of their seats and ran to the altar area, cheerfully desiring to sow into the glory. Our tithes, offerings, and seed should always be presented to the Lord with a cheerful spirit and happiness of heart.

As these people sowed into the glory, many experienced money multiplying in their pockets, purses, wallets, and even within the pages of their Bibles. Several people shared testimonies about the Lord multiplying the last of their money, causing new twenty-, fifty-, and even one hundred-dollar bills to appear where there had been no money. At least ten people experienced the multiplication of twenty-dollar bills that night. It was astonishing.

Bobby Deer, from Quaqtaq, Nunavik, was filming the meeting that night from the back of the sanctuary. When the spirit of generosity quickened the hearts of God's people, Bobby stopped his camera, ran to the altar, and emptied his wallet, knowing God was working miracles. By the time he got back to the video camera, it felt like his wallet had enlarged within his pocket. When he checked to see if money had supernaturally appeared, he was stunned to discover fifteen hundred dollars inside his billfold. He praised the Lord.

I don't understand how these miracles happen. If I could figure it out in my natural mind, it wouldn't be a miracle. That is the wonder of what the Spirit is doing in the earth. He releases His possibilities into the midst of our impossibilities. Every time we have an opportunity to be generous, we're given a divine appointment with blessing, favor, and increase. Sowing into the glory always yields the greatest returns.

> THAT IS THE WONDER OF WHAT THE SPIRIT IS DOING IN THE EARTH. HE RELEASES HIS POSSIBILITIES INTO THE MIDST OF OUR IMPOSSIBILITIES.

## DIVINE TRANSFERENCE OF WEALTH

*"A sinner's wealth is stored up for the righteous."*  (Proverbs 13:22)

Just as Isaiah prophesied, the Spirit wants to give you: *"Hidden treasures, riches stored in secret places, so that you may know that I am the LORD"* (Isaiah 45:3). The Spirit knows where every lost treasure exists in the earth. He sees the hidden drug money, the forgotten inheritance stored behind walls and in attic ceilings, and the golden coins sunk in the depths of the sea. I believe that, somehow, He is able to transfer this wealth from one place to another. If God could supernaturally transport Philip (a living, breathing human of flesh and bones) from one location to another (see Acts 8:39–40), it shouldn't be difficult to believe He can move paper money from the wicked to the righteous.

One summer, as we ministered in Auckland, New Zealand, with Pastors David and Judi Collins, there was a wonderful night when financial miracles took place in the meeting. A realm opened up, and people got out of their seats and became extravagant in their giving. Some were led to sow seed into other people's lives, while others put their money into the offering baskets. As one pastor gave his last fifty dollars, another person was directed to go to him and sow a seed of a thousand dollars into his life. It was awesome! People were led by the Spirit and chose to operate in a generous level of faith, anointing, and glory.

As that realm continued to build, I prophesied into the atmosphere and declared that financial miracles were taking place in people's homes, ministries, and bank accounts. I also prophesied that the Spirit would supernaturally deposit money into somebody's bank account. This was a bold declaration, but the Scriptures tell us that God watches over His Word to perform it. (See Jeremiah 1:12.) Sure enough, the next day we learned that two different ladies had received unexplainable bank account deposits. One received thirty-eight thousand dollars, and the other received forty-one thousand dollars.

This was something new for us, but this miracle testimony became a catalyst for the same thing to happen in countless other places as we shared this testimony in cities around the world. As a result, many others have received supernatural bank account deposits and unexplainable blessings.

During a time of ministry in Ashland, Virginia, on a Saturday night, I presented an opportunity for people to sow into the glory. One dear lady from New York came forward, excitedly bringing a sacrificial financial seed to sow. She had been trying to pay off her daughter's student loan, but the financial burden had weighed on her immensely. She was ready for God to do a miracle in this regard. After sowing her seed, she stood in the glory for a while, her arms lifted to heaven, worshiping in the glory, and allowing that realm to consume her completely. She later wrote me a letter, telling what God had done:

> Brother Joshua, after worshiping in the glory, I went back to my room and opened some mail. I had a letter stating that the final $19,284.39 of my daughter's student loan had been canceled, and I was released from all debt!

These are the kinds of miracles that happen in this realm.

As I received an offering in Honolulu, Hawaii, at the Spiritual Hunger Conference with John and Linda Keough and Cal and Michele Pierce, a woman felt led to give the last of her money. It was like the widow's mite. She knew there wasn't much in her bank account, but she wanted to give all that she had. As the offering was being received, she called the bank to ask for her balance amount, so that she could write a check without overdrawing the account. From the phone call, she learned that several thousand dollars had recently been deposited into her account. These funds, previously denied to her, were somehow unexpectedly released and deposited into her account. It was enough to cover her son's tuition. She loudly rejoiced, praised, and danced with her offering in hand.

This woman had been praying for a breakthrough. Trusting God with her finances caused the miracle to come into her life. It turned into seedtime and harvest time at the same time. *"'The days are coming,' declares the* LORD, *'when the reaper will be overtaken by the plowman and the planter by the one treading grapes. New wine will drip from the mountains and flow from all the hills'"* (Amos 9:13).

Miracles happen quickly in the glory because it is the realm of eternity. When you sow into the glory realm, you reap from that realm of unlimited potential.

And you must understand that when the prosperity of God shows up in your life, it's not just financial blessings that increase. It's miracles for spirit, soul, and body. Right now, reach into the glory, and receive your impartation. Spiritual wheels are turning, and these realms are working together for you.

As the glory changes you, it also changes your outcomes. The Spirit works in you, causing all things to work together for your benefit. This revelation is imparted to you in order for a manifestation to come forth from you. Open your eyes to see dimensions of blessing that you've never seen before. Move toward them. As you do, you walk into favor in unprecedented ways.

The Spirit increases your capacity to receive as you move in the glory. Allow Him to lift you in the Spirit past your current situation and carry you into your promises. Leave the old hindrances in the past. Open wide to your glorious future in God.

Are you hungry to go deeper in the Spirit? He has greater things prepared for you as you determine to enter into these *Glory Realms*.

# 8

# REALMS OF SPIRIT TRAVEL

*Then the Spirit lifted me up and brought me into the inner court,*
*and the glory of the LORD filled the temple.*
—Ezekiel 43:5

**W**hen we speak about moving in the glory, we must also consider the supernatural ways in which the glory moves us! Years ago, I was preparing to step up to the podium to minister at Calvary Campground, in Ashland, Virginia. But as I was being introduced by the camp director, Jane Lowder, the Spirit of prophecy came upon her, and she uttered these words:

> Brother Joshua, God is turning the page, and a new chapter is coming forth. You may say, "I have heard that before," but God says, "I am going to take out some of the old chapters so that you can't even review them. I am taking you into something brand new that you have never been in. Not only will you take it to where you have been, but you will take it to places you've never even thought of.

> "I am going to give you a journey, and you are not going to take it by train or plane or by walking or by donkey or ship. For I shall take you on a journey by My Spirit. Thou shalt see thyself in other countries ministering. Even as thou shalt see it and know it, it shall also be in a natural sort of way.

> "I am still translating people and carrying them forth unto designated areas to minister. I am going to take you on a journey, and you will know that you have been on this journey.

Thou shalt even come back with evidence that thou hast been there."

The Lord says, "Give Me permission to take out the old, so that I can put in the new chapters."

That prophetic word opened a new realm in the Spirit for me, and I have been discovering its possibilities ever since. The Spirit patiently waits for us to discover the exciting possibilities available as we are translated and transported in the supernatural realm. There is a difference between translation and divine translocation. If you are out of the body, it's a translation experience. If you are in the body, it's transportation by the Spirit.

When you are translated in the Spirit, God can move your spirit into past, present, or even future events. In this encounter, your spirit-man is caught up into a supernatural experience. Your spirit may visit the third heaven, or it may visit other locations here on earth. You can fly over nations, into government buildings, or into the midst of important situations to minister to people in need. As your spirit travels, your physical body remains where it is. However, sometimes you will be seen. Your physical body, of course, is not there, but people will see your spirit-body and think it is physical. At other times, you will visit places and be totally invisible.

One of the first times I shared this revelation, there was a woman in the meetings who had been called to go to India to teach a Bible school class for Indian students. She was not strong physically and wondered if she could actually make the trip. While I ministered the Word and revealed these truths, she was lifted out of her body in the Spirit and carried to India. When she appeared before the Indian students, they were surprised because they had not received any advanced notice of her coming. She taught them of the glory and was soon back in her body. Next, she went to Malaysia. Then she traveled to someplace in the Himalayas. She went to all of these places and completed her work during the course of our meeting, before I finished ministering.

When something like this happens, we don't have to worry about where we are going or how to get there because the Spirit is in charge.

As you yield to the Spirit, He takes you where He wills. Translation is never a self-initiated event. It is God who initiates these experiences, and it is God who directs them. Your spirit-man, however, is very active and can be trained to be alert to the ways the Spirit is moving. Our role is simply to yield to Him.

A few years later, I ministered at a conference in Auckland, New Zealand. Just before I began speaking, I felt impressed to pray for Pastor Ian Johnson, a wonderful minister with a great prophetic anointing. As soon as I laid my hands on him, he fell into a deep spiritual trance and was transported to Portugal.

While there, Pastor Ian sat with a man named Russell who was an English minister working in the northern area of Portugal. He was discouraged and thinking about leaving the ministry. But the Spirit sent Pastor Ian there to pray with him, and Russell was greatly encouraged. Again, all of this happened in the course of our meeting.

A short while later, Russell invited Pastor Ian back to Portugal, and he went. They experienced an outpouring of glory, including a massive glory cloud that rolled in over one of the meetings. These are things that only God can do.

It is possible to have supernatural experiences every day as you let the Spirit direct your footsteps. (See Psalm 37:23.) When we think of footsteps, we picture them in the natural with their limitations. They can only reach the length of our natural stride, but in the Spirit, there is no such limitation. One footstep can be in America, and the very next footstep could be in the Congo. One footstep could be in Canada, the next in Australia, the next in Brazil, the next in Egypt, and the next in Mongolia. You can be carried places in intercession, and you can be carried places in the Spirit as you walk by faith.

## WALK, RUN, SOAR!

The prophet Isaiah said:

*But they that wait upon the LORD shall renew their strength; they shall mount up with wings as eagles; they shall run, and not be weary; and they shall walk, and not faint.* (Isaiah 40:31 KJV)

In Isaiah, we are promised supernatural strength to walk the journey ahead, power to run the race, and divine elevation. We need to learn how to obtain this amazing promise. Notice the three dimensions mentioned here: walking, running, and soaring. This promise is for those whose hope is in the Spirit, those who trust in Him, those who wait upon Him (just as a waiter would wait on you at a restaurant), those who pursue the presence of the divine, and those who have their complete devotion focused heavenward. These are the people who will discover their wings.

The promise is that they will *"walk and not faint,"* as well as *"run and not grow weary."* But it goes even further. It says that they will *"mount up with wings as eagles."* I like that, because if we can fly, we can get places faster than we could by walking or running. I spend a lot of time on airplanes, because if you're traveling by car, you go a lot slower and it takes a lot longer to get where you need to go.

Chickens have wings that are big enough and strong enough for them to fly to the highest heights. They should be able to fly with ease, but chickens don't realize that. Their mind tells them they cannot fly, and if you think you can't fly, then you can't. The longest recorded flight of a chicken was thirteen seconds and the longest recorded distance flown was approximately three hundred feet.[1] That's not very long or very far. Chickens just peck around all day, looking for things to eat. They do pause to lay eggs, but that's about the extent of their venture-less life.

But if a dog comes near, or some other predator gets into the chicken coop, the chicken receives new vigor. It suddenly takes wing and flies. True, it doesn't fly any farther than necessary, just enough to escape danger, but it does fly.

That is the image of the average believer, only taking spiritual flight for short distances when danger gets too close, then quickly going back to the mundane status quo of walking in the flesh. Don't be a chicken! You were made to soar in the Spirit! You have wings like an eagle. Spread those wings and fly. Do it often and for long distances. See how far you can go, and enjoy the view from up there.

Eagles have an exceptionally wide wingspan. The wingspan of the bald eagle, for example, is about eight feet and helps them stay in the air for long periods. An eagle flaps his wings to get started in flight, but once he gets high in the air, he moves from working to resting. With his wings spread wide, the air currents carry him. And that's what God calls us to do in the glory.

The Scriptures say that we can walk and not faint (see Galatians 5:16–18), we can run and not be weary (see Elijah in 1 Kings 18:46), and we can fly on wings like eagles. Many of us have used a dimension of faith for walking and the power of the Spirit's anointing for running. Now we're accessing the all-encompassing realms of God's glory to lift us from place to place. Now is the moment to give yourself fully to this realm.

Flapping our wings under the power of God might be likened to the place of anointing. It is God who enables us to flap our wings, and we thank Him for that. But He gives us the ability to labor until we enter into the rest. So, be like the eagle. That's what you were designed for. Soaring on the currents gets you much farther than just flapping your wings and takes a lot less effort on your part, as you learn to yield.

> IT'S EASY TO BECOME TIRED FROM DOING THE SAME OLD THING. THAT'S WHY THE SPIRIT HAS OPENED UP THIS FURTHER DIMENSION, SO WE CAN RISE HIGHER IN THE GLORY.

Many believers become weary from the constant effort they put forth, walking by faith and running with the anointing, but God said, *"Let us not become weary in doing good"* (Galatians 6:9) and *"Never tire of doing what is good"* (2 Thessalonians 3:13). It's easy to become tired from doing the same old thing. That's why the Spirit has opened up this further dimension, so we can rise higher in the glory. Rest in the promise of Isaiah 40. Find yourself in that Scripture and be reenergized.

## FINDING YOUR SPIRIT WINGS

*Fear and trembling overwhelm me, and I can't stop shaking. Oh, that I had wings like a dove; then I would fly away and rest! I would fly far away to the quiet of the wilderness.* (Psalm 55:5–7 NLT)

King David penned those pensive and prophetic words while agonizing over the betrayal and treachery of his trusted counselor and rebellious son. Those he loved most had let him down terribly, and he yearned for an escape. He longed to have wings that would enable him to fly away and find rest.

Maybe you've found yourself feeling the same way. If so, I've got good news for you. God has given you wings. We're not eagles, but we can move about on wings like an eagle. You may not feel like you have wings, but you do. We are redeemed human beings to whom God has given the means to fly.

You have wings, whether you have been soaring or not. I want you to see them now in the Spirit. Close your eyes and picture yourself with big beautiful wings that are divinely connected to your back. Your wings are not small but broad. Your wings are just like the eagle's, majestic and created for spiritual flight.

You might even notice the color, pattern, and texture of your wings. Those wings will lift you to places you've never gone before. They will take you from running victory laps to soaring above your problems altogether. You're being lifted above every situation that threatens to hinder your spiritual growth and progressing toward higher heights of knowing the Spirit. Your *Lifter* is lifting you up so that you can soar. (See Psalm 3:3 KJV.)

## CARRIED AWAY IN THE SPIRIT

Ezekiel had some strange visions. He said:

*I looked, and I saw a windstorm coming out of the north—an immense cloud with flashing lightning and surrounded by brilliant light. The center of the fire looked like glowing metal, and in the fire was what looked like four living creatures. In appearance their form was human, but each of them had four faces and four wings. Their legs were straight; their feet were like those of a calf and gleamed like burnished bronze. Under their wings on their four sides they had human hands. All four of them had faces and wings, and the wings of one touched the wings of another. Each one went straight ahead; they did not turn as they moved.* (Ezekiel 1:4–9)

As Ezekiel looked upon these angelic cherubim, he noticed many things, but what drew his attention most was their wings. He saw *"under their wings,"* and *"the wings of one touched the wings of another,"* as well as *"heard the sound of their wings."* Then, *"When they stood still, they lowered their wings"* (verse 24). What was happening? Ezekiel entered a revelatory place of seeing in the glory. His eyes were opened in the Spirit, and he saw things he had never seen before. Because of this, something began to happen inside of him. Vision always precedes provision.

By the third chapter, Ezekiel was still in the vision and having wonderful encounters with the Spirit. There he said:

> *Then the Spirit lifted me up, and I heard behind me a loud rumbling sound as the glory of the LORD rose from the place where it was standing. It was the sound of the wings of the living creatures brushing against each other and the sound of the wheels beside them, a loud rumbling sound.* (Ezekiel 3:12–13)

The Lifter lifted Ezekiel, and the prophet heard something new. Get ready to see new things and hear new things as the Spirit lifts you.

Next, the Spirit took Ezekiel away:

> *The Spirit then lifted me up and took me away, and I went in bitterness and in the anger of my spirit, with the strong hand of the LORD on me. I came to the exiles who lived at Tel Aviv near the Kebar River. And there, where they were living, I sat among them for seven days—deeply distressed.* (verses 14–15)

Ezekiel went from seeing the living creatures and noticing the sound and movement of their wings, to having their wings come upon him. They lifted him up and carried him into a situation where he was overpowered by the glory of the vision he was witnessing.

Ezekiel was overwhelmed with grief for the sins and miseries of his people, but also because the Spirit of God had come upon him, lifted him up, and literally moved him from one place to another place. There was so much going on all at once!

When you move in the Spirit this way, you may be carried into unpleasant situations or places. You may see things that you wish you had never seen. Even though Ezekiel was deeply distressed by the vision, it was of great importance for him as a prophet. God may show you things in order for you to prophesy and bring divine alignment into a given situation.

## SEEING GOD'S WILL

*The hand of the LORD was on me, and he brought me out by the Spirit of the LORD and set me in the middle of a valley.* (Ezekiel 37:1)

In Ezekiel 37, the Spirit lifted the prophet into the vision of the valley of dry bones. This time, Ezekiel did not see something that existed on the earth or in heaven. Instead, he saw God's will, God's intent for life, and His desire for a region and a people group. This is something that He can also do for you. He might show you such things concerning your family, your business, your community, or your nation.

During his encounter, Ezekiel was called on to prophesy to the dry bones. As you travel in the Spirit, expect there to be times when God calls on you to prophesy. In that moment, you will be made to understand the will of God, and you can then decree it. Things can change in a moment as you speak. There have been times when I've flown over nations, and the Lord gave me one word to decree. I've spoken it and seen the manifestation of it come to pass quickly.

> AS YOU TRAVEL IN THE SPIRIT, EXPECT THERE TO BE TIMES WHEN GOD CALLS ON YOU TO PROPHESY. IN THAT MOMENT, YOU WILL BE MADE TO UNDERSTAND THE WILL OF GOD, AND YOU CAN THEN DECREE IT.

For instance, I was in Glasgow, Scotland, and spoke the words "supernatural debt cancellation." I had seen it in the Spirit, and told the people in Glasgow that it wasn't just an individual blessing, but something that would come to the nation. The very next day the newspapers reported that £220 million of consumer debt was being canceled.[2] Needless to say, this positively affected the very people who had heard me decree it the night before.

Something similar happened when I was in Colombo, Sri Lanka. After I spoke a word of national blessing I had been given in the Spirit realm, immediately the local stock markets rose. You can accelerate at an unprecedented pace when you're soaring in the Spirit.

As I write these words, I'm sitting on a transcontinental flight from San Francisco to London. The screen in front of me indicates that we're traveling at the remarkable speed of 657 mph. At this rate, it will take just over nine hours to reach my destination from one continent to another. But in the Spirit, we can travel even faster.

Recently, while visiting Durban, South Africa, I was lifted in the Spirit and taken on a global tour. My spirit flew faster than any jet. I felt as though I was a shooting star, zipping from place to place. I went from Africa, back to America, then to the Middle East, to Europe, across Asia, and back to Africa. In each location, the Spirit directed my spirit in intercession and ministry. The whole trip did not take more than an hour in the natural, and yet so much was accomplished in the Spirit during that time. The glory accelerates our usefulness.

## HOW TO DISCERN THE REALM

Just because you've never heard of something before doesn't mean that it's not from God. Just because you've never experienced something before doesn't mean that it's not from Him. Do you think you know everything that God has said? Do you think you've seen everything that God has done? This is where the discerning of spirits comes in, for we must discern the source of every miracle and revelation.

And how do we discern these realms? We discern what something is by the fruit it produces: *"A good tree cannot bear bad fruit, and a bad tree cannot bear good fruit"* (Matthew 7:18). This makes it much easier to discern the good from the bad. We can also ask the following questions: Is it contradictory to the Scriptures? Does it lower Jesus Christ from the Godhead? Does it glorify God? Put every spiritual encounter to the test. If you discern that it is from God, then receive it and refuse to back away from it.

## NIGHT ENCOUNTERS

*I slept but my heart was awake.*                    (Song of Solomon 5:2)

Why do many translation experiences occur at night? During the nighttime we are in a totally relaxed state in our bodies. This allows our spirit-man to be more sensitive to the leading of the Spirit. God's people can be used to do great things even while they sleep.

Many of our clearest dreams are a result of traveling in the Spirit. This is certainly not true of all dreams, but the details of some dreams are so vivid, so real, and so alive that they may be the result of your spirit traveling in the glory as you sleep. It may seem like a dream, but it may actually be much more than a dream.

There have been times when I was carried away in the Spirit. I saw things then came back and had to think very hard, *Was that a dream or did I really go there and minister in that way last night?* Many times, I concluded that I actually went and ministered in the way I had dreamed about it. The proof has been the countless individuals from all around the world who shared their experiences of seeing me minister in a certain location or having specific interactions with me that never occurred in an earthly manner.

There is a great difference in the ministry when the Spirit of God carries you away. He uses you, but does all the work. At times, you might feel a jolt as you're falling asleep. This often indicates your spirit-man leaving your body. The jolt is a physical reaction of fear attempting to stop the process. With spirit separation, your body thinks you are dying. Fear will block you from moving in the Spirit. Rebuke it, embrace God's love, and move on.

In some of our dreams, we are perched on the edge of a building or a high cliff, getting ready to thrust ourselves out to soar. These, too, may be spiritual experiences. Go ahead and fly. Some people dream of falling and wake up terrified. When anything like this happens, pray, "Spirit, I give myself to You. I am not afraid of Your leading, I am not afraid of Your glory, and I yield to Your divine translation. I yield to traveling in the Spirit, for I trust You." Once you do this, instead of feeling afraid, you will find God's peace in order to enjoy the journey. You might even find yourself going into these experiences more and more.

This is an important point. The Scriptures say, *"For those who are led by the Spirit of God are the children of God"* (Romans 8:14). As the sons and daughters of God, we must be willing to be led at all times in all locations. Let us become more sensitive to the guidance and direction of the Spirit.

> AS THE SONS AND DAUGHTERS OF GOD, WE MUST BE WILLING TO BE LED AT ALL TIMES IN ALL LOCATIONS. LET US BECOME MORE SENSITIVE TO THE GUIDANCE AND DIRECTION OF THE SPIRIT.

After having an experience of Spirit translation, you may or may not remember the location, the people, or the circumstances. Then, days, weeks, months, or even years later, something happens that triggers a memory. Many people dismiss it as déjà vu because they're in a situation that feels as if they've been there before. That's because they have. As I noted earlier, in a translation experience, the Spirit sometimes shows you the future. When you actually live that real-time experience, you realize you have been there before.

But why would we be shown something from the future? Perhaps it's to get us ready for what's to come. Perhaps it's to make us more sensitive to the Spirit's working so that we can accomplish His will. Whatever the purpose, when you get the sense that you have been there before, thank God that He has miraculously prepared you for that exact moment in time.

What many call déjà vu is what John the Revelator was speaking about in Revelation 4:1, when the Spirit called him up and showed him things to come. Prepare yourself in the nighttime hours by keeping a pen and paper at your bedside, ready to record these experiences. When John came out of his encounter, he had a new revelation. You can have a new revelation too.

## TRANSLATED IN THE CANADIAN ARCTIC

Paul said, *"In the body or out of the body I do not know"* (2 Corinthians 12:2). Paul wasn't sure if he was translated or not, but knew he had been caught up to the third heaven. There, he experienced God and received revelation. Whether it happened in or out of the body wasn't important.

The same may happen to you. Remember, if you are out of the body, it's a translation experience. If you are in the body, it's transportation by the Spirit.

Some years ago, I was translated in the Spirit while on an airplane. We took off from Iqaluit, Nunavut, the capital city on Baffin Island in the Canadian Arctic. I was on my way to minister to the Inuit people (most people know them as Eskimos) in Qikiqtarjuaq, a small community further north in the Arctic Circle. Before I knew what was happening, I was carried away in the Spirit and lifted up over the land of the Canadian North.

As I looked down upon the whole region, I saw a layer of darkness covering it. As I watched, I saw the hand of the Lord holding a rake. He took this rake and worked it back and forth across the land, removing the layer of darkness. The entire area was revealed as a pure, glistening white blanket of snow.

Next, tiny golden sprouts grew through the white snow, until the whole land was covered with golden vegetation: flowers, fruit and vegetable plants, and trees of all kinds. I asked the Lord, "What does this mean?" He lowered me toward the earth and instructed me to take an ear of golden corn from a stalk in front of me, which I did. Instead of finding corn kernels inside as I peeled back the husk, there were beautifully arranged diamonds, fixed neatly in rows.

I asked the Lord, "Why?"

He responded by saying, "My abundance comes as my Spirit and truth is revealed and accepted."

At that moment, I shot back into my physical body. I opened my eyes and saw that we were pulling into the airport terminal in Qikiqtarjuaq. My traveling companion was shaking me and saying, "Joshua! Joshua, are you okay? Are you okay? Are you okay?" Apparently, he thought I had died, when, in reality, I had been lifted out of my body for a time.

He later told me that it was the most turbulent flight he had ever been on. Passengers screamed. Things fell everywhere. The pilot was able to land the plane safely, and that's when I came back into my body. Now I had a message. God had shown me His intent for the people there, but I had not experienced any of the perils of the flight, none of the turbulence and none of the terror the other passengers had experienced. Because of this encounter, I was able to go into those meetings in the Arctic with a clear vision of God's purpose and a clear message from Him.

At the time, I considered this to be a wonderful, once-in-a-lifetime experience. Because of the vision and message God had given me, I fell deeply in love with the Inuit people. Over the next two years, I made twenty-seven trips from one side of the Arctic to the other, ministering wherever the Spirit opened new doors, establishing lasting friendships and seeing the manifestation of the things that God had shown me in the Spirit.

If I had looked at that situation in the natural, I probably never would have gone back. There was not much there except cold tundra and polar bears (no trees or other vegetation), but the people were so beautiful. I sensed God's great love for them and knew His promise was to prosper them. Soon, we heard reports about berries growing where they had never grown before. Clams were harvested from the waters where there had never been any before. People discovered veins of silver and gold in the hills. They found diamonds—a lot of diamonds. *Time* magazine carried an article about the diamonds discovered in what had always been considered a wasteland in the Canadian Arctic, and described how this discovery was changing the lives of aboriginal people.[3] God redeemed the land and blessed the people because of His glory. He brought His prosperity and provision out of that once desolate land.

This experience was significant and pivotal to our ministry. I believe God has encounters for you that will be just as pivotal and just as significant for the places He has prepared for you to go.

## TRANSPORTED BY THE SPIRIT

Again, transportation by the Spirit is different from translation in the Spirit. With transportation, the physical body is lifted into a supernatural experience in which a person (or group of people or objects) travels from one place to another without the confinements of time or distance. In a mere second, like a flash, you can move to another location on the planet, bypassing all natural restraints.

Unlike translation, when you travel by transportation by the Spirit, your physical body will always be noticeable to those around you. Wherever you go, you will be seen. Often, people will not even realize that you have been supernaturally transported into the given situation, knowing nothing of what has taken place. It will seem natural to others, although you may need to overcome fear and shock on your part. You will appear fully in your human form, but are there supernaturally, on a mission sent by the Spirit for a specific purpose.

Elijah apparently had a reputation for travel in the Spirit. When Elijah met Obadiah, Obadiah said to him, "'*But now you tell me to go to my master and say, 'Elijah is here.' I don't know where the Spirit of the* LORD *may carry you when I leave you. If I go and tell Ahab and he doesn't find you, he will kill me*" (1 Kings 18:11–12).

Obadiah had a situation on his hands. He knew that the Spirit of God was on Elijah and was afraid that if he left Elijah, the Spirit would transport Elijah somewhere else. Then Obadiah's master, whom he had told that Elijah had come, would think he was a fool, and Obadiah would have to answer for it. What an amazing problem to have! These are not fairy tales or some sort of myth.

It happened to Philip: "*When they came up out of the water, the Spirit of the Lord suddenly took Philip away, and the eunuch did not see him again, but went on his way rejoicing*" (Acts 8:39).

This was a *suddenly*, and that's how translation in the Spirit and transportation by the Spirit happens—suddenly. One minute, Philip was baptizing the Ethiopian eunuch. Then the Spirit of God came on him. The next verse shows us: "*Philip, however, appeared at Azotus and traveled about, preaching the gospel in all the towns until he reached Caesarea*" (verse 40). Philip was one place baptizing an Ethiopian who had believed, when quite suddenly he was lifted up and appeared somewhere else. I looked up these two locations and found that the distance between them was twenty-five miles.

Some people, trying to belittle the supernatural, insist that Philip just walked away because he had finished his ministry in that first place. But the Greek word *harpazo*, which was translated into English here as "*took...away*," means "to seize, catch away, pluck, pull or take away by force." So, Philip did not just walk away. The Spirit came upon him and plucked him up, taking him by force, and supernaturally transporting his body twenty-five miles down the road.

Something similar happened to Jesus in Luke 24:31, when He vanished from the sight of two men who were on their way to Emmaus: *"Then their eyes were opened and they recognized him, and he disappeared from their sight."*

## CARS, BOATS, AND OTHER OBJECTS TRANSPORTED

Can you be transported while driving in your car? Yes! It has happened to us a number of times, once when traveling with our entire ministry team. We had been in Burbank, California, making preparations for an event we were to do there at a later date. We headed out to Ontario, California, when something supernatural happened. We got stuck in rush-hour traffic that was backed up so far it seemed we would never get through. We prayed, and the next exit sign we saw said Vineyard Avenue, which is in Ontario. That trip should have taken an hour or more, but only ten or fifteen minutes had elapsed on the clock. In the natural, that's impossible, but in the Spirit all things are possible.

Some have asked me, "Is that scriptural? Where is it in the Bible?" I'm so glad they asked and was ready with an answer. John 6:21 says, *"Then they were willing to take him* [Jesus] *into the boat, and immediately the boat reached the shore where they were heading."* It was approximately two miles across the sea to the other shore, and it normally took some time to cross. This time, however, they were there *immediately.* So, Jesus was transported, the disciples were transported, and the boat they were in was transported.

Not only can the Spirit supernaturally move people, but it can also move objects, finances, missing items—the possibilities are unlimited! Amazing! That's what happens when you are transported in the Spirit.

## TRANSPORTED OVERSEAS

Quite a few years ago, I was ministering at an Assemblies of God church in Pensacola, Florida. I had finished my sermon, and began moving in words of knowledge and praying for the various needs of the people. Then something amazing happened. One moment I was in Pensacola, Florida, with my hands raised, believing God for others, and the next moment, when I opened my eyes, I was in a foreign place surrounded by unfamiliar people. They were in front of me, behind me, pressed in on both sides of me, all of us squished together in a tiny elevator.

I looked around and tried to figure out what I was supposed to be doing. A pang of fear hit me. Questions rushed through my mind: *Why am I here? How will I get back to my family in Florida? I'm supposed to be speaking in Florida. What's going on?* I didn't know the language being spoken. All I knew was to speak in tongues, and that's what I did.

I got off the elevator and found my way out of the front doors of the building. Walking down the street, I realized it was morning. Although I had never been here before, I recognized the place from photos I had seen in books and magazines. For months, I had prayed for this specific communist nation, laying hands on my map at home. Now I stood in that land.

I asked the Lord for His supernatural leading. He was faithful and directed me by His Spirit. Walking farther down the street, I found myself at what looked like an office building. I walked inside without being questioned. By following the leading of the Spirit, I came upon a group of believers who were gathered to pray.

I joined their prayer meeting, even though I didn't understand any of the language. I prayed in tongues and knew God had me there for a reason not yet clear to me. The prayers of the people were powerful, and God used this time to shift things in the atmosphere. I received an impartation that would open doors of opportunity by standing among these people by divine appointment. Although unable to communicate what was happening to me with the people, I had some business cards in my pocket. I handed a card to one of the men at the gathering, and he gave me his in exchange.

When I sensed that my time there was complete, my faith told me to get back to the same elevator in which I had arrived, and that's what I did. It might sound funny, but Jesus said, *"According to your faith be it unto you"* (Matthew 9:29 KJV). That's where my faith was stationed, so there, in that elevator, I lifted my hands, shut my eyes, and praised the Lord. Suddenly, I was back in the church in Pensacola, standing in the same place I had been when I left. The glory was thick, and I couldn't speak. Such experiences produce an awe of the power of the Spirit.

To my utter surprise, a few weeks later, I received an email from a pastor in the country I had just supernaturally visited, thanking me for coming and being a part of their gathering. He welcomed me back anytime. A few months before this writing, I had the privilege of returning to that same place, this time arriving by airplane. I can tell you this, although the idea might cause mild trembling to some, supernatural transport is a much better and an incomprehensibly quicker way to travel!

While in that country this time, I met with a lady who had been in that small prayer group the day the Spirit transported me overseas. She hadn't realized that it was a supernatural occurrence and thought I had come in some natural way. That's how it seems to others around you when the Spirit lifts you in this manner.

Since that time, I've discovered there were several reasons the Spirit carried me to that foreign nation in such an unusual and profound way. Joshua 1:3 says that He will give us every place our foot treads upon. I had been praying for that communist country The Spirit lifted me and set me down there, so my feet would touch the soil and give me spiritual possession of the promise. Let God lift you into your promises.

After this happened, I received countless invitations from all across that country to come and minister the good news of the gospel. Only eternity will tell the fullness of this testimony, but one thing is certain: the Spirit knows how to make a way for you!

## WALKING THROUGH WALLS AND WALKING INTO HEAVEN

In John 20:19, Jesus appeared to the disciples, even though the doors had been locked for fear that those who had killed Him would try to kill them too. Those locked doors didn't stop Jesus; He just walked right through them. His disciples were amazed, but Jesus came to give them a revelatory message, saying, *"Peace be with you! As the Father has sent me, I am sending you"* (John 20:21). If Jesus was transported, and He is our example, we should trust for this miracle too.

Hebrews 11:5–6 speaks of the faith of Enoch and of him being transported. He was *"taken from this life"* (verse 5). Genesis 5:24 says it this way: *"Enoch walked faithfully with God; then he was no more, because God took him away."* How was Enoch taken away? He was transported by the Spirit. He walked with God, and then God said, "Come with Me." Just like that, Enoch was whisked away, lifted up, pulled up, and caught away into the realm of the eternal.

Are you hungry to go deeper in the Spirit? He has greater things prepared for you as you determine to enter into these *Glory Realms*.

# 9

# REALMS OF HEAVENLY ENCOUNTER

*By faith Abraham, when called to go to a place he would*
*later receive as his inheritance, obeyed and went,*
*even though he did not know where he was going.*
—Hebrews 11:8

One of the joys (and major sacrifices) I've had to make in order to fulfill the call of God upon my life is to spend time in foreign lands among strangers in unfamiliar places. I spend more than half my life away from home, as I have since I was in my early twenties. Everywhere I've gone, the Spirit has led me by divine connection to establish new friendships. I have thousands of stories about the extraordinary things I've experienced and seen.

I've been escorted through the hallways of parliamentary and government buildings to pray and release the glory there. I've sung at presidential gatherings and attended exclusive Hollywood events in order to privately minister to those in the upper echelons of society. As a child, I never dreamed that I would stand on the Great Wall of China, take an elevator to the top of the Eiffel Tower, crawl inside the Great Pyramid of Giza, or trek through the mystical wilderness of Easter Island, and yet, I've had the opportunity to do all of these things. But, just as Dorothy said in *The Wizard of Oz*, "There's no place like home." Nothing compares to being in my own country, spending time in my own house, driving my own car, eating my own familiar food, and spending time with the family I love so dearly.

To be honest, sometimes I start missing my home even before I've taken the first leg of an overseas trip. Undoubtedly, God has given me a special grace for the call. But there are still times when I've only been gone a few days, yet feel an unquenchable longing to hold my wife and give my children a good hug.

Isn't it the same in the realms of the Spirit? We travel through this earthly life with a mandate from God to win the lost, heal the sick, and bring deliverance to the captives. But we're homesick, because our real home is a heavenly one. There's such a desire within us to go deeper in the things of God, knowing we were created for much more. Hebrews continues to speak of Abraham:

> By faith he made his home in the promised land like a stranger in a foreign country; he lived in tents, as did Isaac and Jacob, who were heirs with him of the same promise. For he was looking forward to the city with foundations, whose architect and builder is God…. And so from this one man, and he as good as dead, came descendants as numerous as the stars in the sky and as countless as the sand on the seashore. (Hebrews 11:9–10, 12)

Then, of a larger list of men and women of faith, Hebrews says:

> All these people were still living by faith when they died. They did not receive the things promised; they only saw them and welcomed them from a distance, admitting that they were foreigners and strangers on earth. (verse 13)

This chapter in the book of Hebrews is a Hall of Faith, a *Who's Who* listing of the great men and women of the Old Testament. Despite their walk of confidence, these great heroes of faith did not receive all their promises on earth, even though they had seen them.

As foreigners and strangers here on earth, we identify with the confession of these men and women of old:

> People who say such things show that they are looking for a country of their own. If they had been thinking of the country they had left, they would have had opportunity to return. Instead, they were longing for a better country—a heavenly one. (verses 14–16)

These passages from Hebrews give us an understanding of the truth that our faith has an eternal purpose, just like the faith of our forefathers. That eternal purpose is the reward of heaven and the blessings of heavenly glory.

As we learn to walk by faith, run with the anointing, and soar in the Spirit, we are rewarded with the privileged opportunity of exploring the various realms of heaven. Men of old didn't see the fullness of their vision here on the earth, but were taken into the heavenly city, which was their reward. Today, as children of a better covenant, we see heaven coming to earth in response to the prayers of Jesus. Our longing for this heavenly homeland creates a suction in the Spirit that pulls those things that are eternal into the realm of natural manifestation.

> TODAY, AS CHILDREN OF A BETTER COVENANT, WE SEE HEAVEN COMING TO EARTH IN RESPONSE TO THE PRAYERS OF JESUS. OUR LONGING FOR THIS HEAVENLY HOMELAND CREATES A SUCTION IN THE SPIRIT THAT PULLS THOSE THINGS THAT ARE ETERNAL INTO THE REALM OF NATURAL MANIFESTATION.

## THE THREE REALMS OF HEAVEN

*But will God really dwell on earth? The heavens* [the first and second heavens], *even the highest heaven* [the third heaven], *cannot contain you. How much less this temple I have built!*

(1 Kings 8:27)

There are three realms of heaven, just as there are three predominant realms in the Spirit. As you've read through this book, I trust that you have captured this revelation, like a heavenly blueprint, to see how these things all work together, creating a progressive whirlwind in the Spirit for us to ascend into the glory realm.

*You alone are the* LORD. *You made the heavens* [the first and second heavens], *even the highest heavens* [the third heaven], *and all their starry host, the earth and all that is on it, the seas and all that is in them. You give life to everything, and the multitudes of heaven worship you.* (Nehemiah 9:6)

*Such a high priest truly meets our need—one who is holy, blameless, pure, set apart from sinners, exalted above the heavens* [the first, second, and third heavens]. (Hebrews 7:26)

The word *heaven* is used nearly seven hundred times in the Bible. Because there are three different heavens, we need to be able to differentiate between them in order to understand fully what the Scriptures give reference to in each case. *"Look, I see the heavens opened and the Son of Man standing in the place of honor at God's right hand!"* (Acts 7:56 NLT)

## THE FIRST HEAVEN

*In the beginning God created the heavens and the earth.*

(Genesis 1:1)

The heaven referenced in the above Scripture could not be God's dwelling place because He is eternal. He always was, always is, and always will be. The realm in which He abides, the glory realm (or the third heaven), is the realm of eternity. Like Him, it always was, always is, and always will be. Therefore, the heaven God created which is mentioned in the first verse of Genesis is another heaven.

Because it is linked together with the creation of the earth, Genesis appears to refer to the heavens immediately above us that surround our planet. The first heaven, scientifically referred to as the troposphere,[1] is the sky above us and the atmosphere of planet Earth. We look up and say, "The heavens are so beautiful today."

When we look up at the clouds and watch the birds fly through the air (see Psalm 104:12 KJV), this is the heaven we see with our natural eyes. This heaven is the domain in which we live, right under this realm of heaven. Revelation 21:1 says, *"Then I saw 'a new heaven and a new earth,' for the **first heaven** and the first earth had passed away."* This was John the Revelator speaking. He was having a series of heavenly encounters. In this one, he saw a new heaven and a new earth. The first heaven and the first earth had passed away.

Some think this first heaven that was destroyed was the heaven where God lived, but that can't be the case. He would never destroy the perfect place of His habitation. He was referring to our atmosphere. So now we understand what the first heaven is.

## THE SECOND HEAVEN

*Then another sign appeared in heaven* [the second heaven]: *an enormous red dragon with seven heads and ten horn, and seven crowns on its heads. Its tail swept a third of the stars from the sky and flung them to the earth.*                    (Revelation 12:3–4)

*The stars of heaven* [the second heaven] *and their constellations will not show their light. The rising sun will be darkened and the moon will not give its light.*                    (Isaiah 13:10)

This heaven is a spiritual realm and the place where the angels of God war against the demonic forces of darkness. The second heaven is where Satan has established his throne and where he governs over the dark angels that joined forces with him in rebellion against God. It is the celestial heaven of outer space. (See Deuteronomy 4:19; Matthew 24:29.) This includes the galaxies, solar systems, and planets that exist just beyond our earthly atmosphere.

In *Young's Literal Translation* of the Scriptures, this heaven is also referred to as *mid-heaven* in Revelation 8:13, 14:6, and 19–17. Why? Because it is in between the first and third heavens. This heaven is the domain of the principalities and rulers of darkness, just as the first heaven is our domain. Isaiah 24:21 says, *"In that day the LORD will punish the powers in the heavens above* [the second heaven] *and the kings on the earth below."* Ephesians 6:12 says, *"For our struggle is not against flesh and blood, but against the rulers, against the authorities, against the powers of this dark world and against the spiritual forces of evil in the heavenly realms."* Those heavenly realms could not possibly be the third heaven where God lives, for the place where He lives is perfect.

In Revelation 14:6, *The Amplified Bible* calls this place midheaven without specifying which heaven it is referring to: *"Then I saw another angel flying in midheaven, with an eternal gospel to preach to the inhabitants of the earth."* Other translations simply say, *"…in the midst of heaven."*

In Daniel 10:13, a messenger angel encountered an angel whom he called *"the prince of the Persian kingdom."* This angel warred with him for twenty-one days until Michael, the warrior angel came to help him. Then, the messenger angel was released to deliver a message to Daniel.

These are the heavenly realms spoken of in Ephesians 6:12, the second heaven. That realm of heaven is dark with much demonic activity. It is the place where Satan and his fallen angels dwell. Thank God, the battle belongs to the Lord, but the blessing belongs to the children of God.

Let's lift our vision a bit higher to see into the realm of the highest heavens.

## THE THIRD HEAVEN

*For Christ did not enter a sanctuary made with human hands that was only a copy of the true one; he entered heaven itself, now to appear for us in God's presence.* (Hebrews 9:24)

This is the glory realm, the dimension of eternal blessings, where there is no sickness, no poverty, no strife, and no warfare. There will be no battles in the third heaven, for it is a realm of peace, of ease, and of rest. The third heaven is the realm above and beyond our universe. I like to call it *beyond beyond,* because we consider the astrological heavens to be *beyond.* So, when we're speaking about going *beyond beyond,* we're prophesying encounters from the realms of the third heaven. This heaven is the abode of God or, what is referred to within the context of the Scriptures as Paradise. (See Luke 23:43; Revelation 2:7.)

Paul spoke of this heaven in 2 Corinthians 12:1, when he said, "*I must go on boasting. Although there is nothing to be gained, I will go on to visions and revelations from the Lord. I know a man in Christ who fourteen years ago was caught up to the third heaven.*" It seems clear that Paul was talking about himself, although he was reluctant to do so.

> WE NEED TO BE CAREFUL HOW MUCH WE SHARE WITH OTHERS ABOUT OUR HEAVENLY ENCOUNTERS.... SOME THINGS THE SPIRIT SHARES WITH YOU ARE FOR YOUR OWN SPIRITUAL JOURNEY AND SHOULD NOT BE SHARED WITH OTHERS.

We need to be careful how much we share with others about our heavenly encounters. Not everyone can receive what the Spirit does for you. Some things the Spirit shares with you are for your own spiritual journey and should not be shared with others.

At other times, God may give you a vision that's important for others to know about. The key is being sensitive to the proper timing and opportunity. Ask the Spirit for a greater sensitivity to see into this realm and for His guidance to properly steward the visions He gives. The glimpses of eternity that the Spirit gives are for us to understand how great God really is. Back in 2 Corinthians, Paul did not want it to be apparent that he was talking about himself. He used the phrase, *"I know a man."* Paul wanted them to know that it wasn't about him; it was about God.

What happened to Paul? He was *"caught up to the third heaven"* where he heard inexpressible and incomprehensible things. This is the only place in the Scriptures where this term, *the third heaven,* is used. However, there are other passages within the Scriptures that give an understanding of the third heaven and show us that it is above the second and first heavens. One of those passages is Psalm 115:16, which states, *"The highest heavens belong to the LORD, but the earth he has given to mankind."* If there are *highest heavens,* then the logical conclusion is that there are also lower heavens. When we navigate in the Spirit we move from faith to anointing to glory. In actuality, we are transitioned from the first heaven into the second heaven and finally into the third heaven.

## YOUR PRAYERS AND THE REALMS OF HEAVEN

> *Your kingdom come, your will be done, on earth as it is in heaven.*
> —Jesus (Matthew 6:10)

When Jesus was on the earth, He taught His disciples how to pray, using a very specific model. The first words of that prayer refer to heaven. When praying, it is important to keep in mind the three realms of heaven. In addition, there is a difference between first-day, second-day, and third-day intercession. First-day intercession deals with the first heaven, or natural world, this place of reason and praying out of logic. Second-day intercession takes you higher, to a place of warring with the spiritual powers, the principalities, and the demonic realm that occupies the second heaven.

Some believers get stuck in their intercession and remain in the logical realm of the first heaven. Instead of praying in the Spirit, they pray from their own minds. These kinds of prayers bring disappointments, unexpected results, and personal discouragement. In this realm, you may feel defeated by the enemy, who comes for one reason: to steal, kill, and destroy, because you're looking at what happens in the natural troposphere. The Greek word *tropo* means "change." The natural dimension is always subject to change.

This is even truer of those who go higher, into the second heaven with their intercession. Since this is a realm where demonic activity dominates, those who pray in this realm are always battling, waging war against the forces of darkness. This is hard work. If you stay in this realm, you will become battle weary. But the Scriptures teach us that the battle belongs to the Lord, for He has already defeated our enemies. (See 1 Samuel 17:47; 2 Chronicles 20:15.) The blessings (spoils) of battle belong to the children of God. In our prayers, He calls us to come higher, not to stay in first heaven or second heaven intercession, but to move up into a third heaven dimension of intercession.

When you get into intercession in this heavenly realm, you see things as they already are in heaven. Then you can use your prayers to move the revelation from heaven into manifestation on the earth.

Matthew 6:9–10 begins the model prayer Jesus taught His disciples. In it, He said, *"This, then, is how you should pray:...your kingdom come, your will be done, on earth as it is in heaven."* That is third-day intercession, and the Spirit gives us an understanding of it now.

> HEAVEN, FOR MOST PEOPLE, IS A MYSTERIOUS PLACE FAR AWAY, BUT WE HAVE THE OPPORTUNITY TO MAKE IT AN INTEGRAL PART OF OUR EVERYDAY LIFE.

Heaven, for most people, is a mysterious place far away, but we have the opportunity to make it an integral part of our everyday life. If Jesus prayed that we would experience these realms of glory while we are still here on the earth, then we can, and we should.

# HEAVEN COMING TO EARTH

*Father, I want those you have given me to be with me where I am, and to see my glory, the glory you have given me because you loved me before the creation of the world.*　　　　　　　　　　　(John 17:24)

What images do you see in your mind when you think about heaven coming to earth? Some people think about angels or the joy and peace of God. Some think about happiness or the brilliant radiance of the Lord's light. Some think about their loved ones who have passed on or the limitless blessings mentioned within the Scriptures. Do you realize that when you think and talk about heaven, heavenly things begin to surround you here? Spiritually speaking, whatever you focus on increases in your life.

If you study what the Scriptures have to say regarding healing, you will see healing power flow in a greater way. If you find all the Scriptures that refer to God's promised blessings and focus on them, it is impossible not to experience a portion of that blessing. It is the same when it comes to the heavenly dimension. The Scriptures have a lot to say about heaven. I believe the Spirit wants to reveal this realm to us more and more.

Recently, more people are experiencing the reality of heaven. This is because our earthly timeline is running out, and eternity is beginning to run in. Some have had visions of Jesus and, through them, became acquainted with the glories of heaven, even walking on the streets of gold.

Heaven, just like Solomon's Temple in Jerusalem, is filled with gold, and there even seems to be a shimmering glory that fills the atmosphere. It should not surprise any of us that the manifestations of God's glory appear tangibly upon people in this way. Gold is part of God's realm. Symbolically, it represents divinity and prosperity.

We have watched this manifestation of glory fall through the air, landing upon us and others as we worship. At other times, it seems to come directly up from the pores of our skin. It can be very fine and shimmers with clear or a multicolored diamond-like appearance. Take a look at your hands right now as you read this. As you look for the glory you will begin to see it. When you see it on your hands, on your face, or on your surroundings, don't be afraid. Be grateful. It is a wonderful foretaste of heaven and a reminder that this heavenly glory flows through your life. This is part of what Jesus prayed for, that we would see the glory of heaven.

## FEASTING IN HEAVEN

*On this mountain the LORD Almighty will prepare a feast of rich food for all peoples, a banquet of aged wine—the best of meats and the finest of wines.* (Isaiah 25:6)

The Scriptures paint a beautiful picture of the feast in heaven, and you can't have a feast without plenty of food. Have you ever wondered about the purpose for eating in heaven? It certainly cannot be for survival, as it is here on earth. Therefore, it must be for growth, an impartation in heavenly food because it's a spiritual substance.

When we partake of the Lord's Supper, we receive by faith, His body that was broken and the new covenant that is in His blood. John the Revelator received an impartation of the Spirit of prophecy when he ate a scroll given to him by an angel. (See Revelation 10:9–11.) Ezekiel was also given scrolls to eat, and this enabled him to speak with boldness. (See Ezekiel 3:1–3.) There were times when I've seen God release scrolls in the Spirit. I knew they came for us to eat in order to receive a fresh impartation.

Sometimes, these scrolls were given with new songs and, at other times, with a word in season, but the scrolls always came with impartation. Don't be afraid to receive what the Spirit gives to you in the glory. At times, I've lifted my hands above my head in a meeting and sensed the denseness of the cloud. By faith, I've touched that realm, and, by the anointing, become aware of what is available. But in the glory, I've received the impartation and allowed God to fill me with His spiritual substance.

**DON'T BE AFRAID TO RECEIVE WHAT THE SPIRIT GIVES TO YOU IN THE GLORY.**

Sometimes, the glory tastes like honey, at other times, like a sweet dessert. While I was ministering in San Diego, California, a realm of God was ushered into the meeting. Corporately, we both tasted and sensed the glory to be like a marshmallow. Many people smelled its candy-sweet aroma, while others physically tasted it in their mouths. Such joy overflowed onto the people with laughter and ecstasy that they even fell out of their seats. This great awareness of God enlarged us in the things of the Spirit. Just like a heated marshmallow expands, God filled us with spiritual substance which was then enlarged by the fire of His Spirit within us.

God never intended that we would just get by or have just enough. He is the God of more than enough! In the glory, God brings us to the place of overflow. Lift your hands into the cloud now. Taste and see that the Lord is good!

## THE ETERNAL REALM

When considering the realms of God's glory, we must realize that God created an eternal dwelling place for all believers in Christ. That includes you and me. The third heaven is the abode of God, but also the place where all believers will live with Him forever. The Scriptures make it clear that we, as believers in Christ Jesus, will never die. We will live eternally with God in the third heaven. Our spirits come from the realm of eternity and are destined to return and live in that realm.

Romans 2:7 says, *"To those who by persistence in doing good seek glory, honor and immortality, he will give eternal life."* Romans 6:22 says, *"But now that you have been set free from sin and have become slaves of God, the benefit you reap leads to holiness, and the result is eternal life."*

What does *eternal life* mean? It simply means you will live forever. Galatians 6:8 says, *"Whoever sows to please their flesh, from the flesh will reap destruction; whoever sows to please the Spirit, from the Spirit will reap eternal life."* Titus 3:7 says, *"So that, having been justified by his grace, we might become heirs having the hope of eternal life."* This wasn't of our own doing, and it wasn't because of our own performance. It was because of His grace that He declared us righteous and gave us the confidence of inheriting eternal life.

## A BELIEVER NEVER DIES

Not only are we being offered glimpses into heaven, but heaven also looks down upon us! We need to change our vocabulary regarding the saints who once lived here on the earth. Too often, we speak of them in the past tense. After all, they died, didn't they? But that can't be right. The Scriptures say that a believer never dies. We just go from one dimension of living into a higher dimension, from one place of walking into a higher place of walking. We just step from one realm into a greater realm. We never truly die.

My body isn't who I am. It's just my earthsuit. I am a spirit, and my spirit will never die. It will go from this realm into the next with ease. So, when talking about the saints who have gone on before us, we should probably say: they passed on, they crossed over, they graduated, or they were upgraded.

We know these saints are a whole lot happier in glory than they ever were here. According to the Scriptures, their bodies have been transformed into bodies that never die. 1 Corinthians 15:53–57 (NLT) says exactly that:

> For our dying bodies must be transformed into bodies that will never die; our mortal bodies must be transformed into immortal bodies. Then, when our dying bodies have been transformed into bodies that will never die, this scripture will be fulfilled: "Death is swallowed up in victory. O death, where is your victory? O death, where is your sting?" For sin is the sting that results in death, and the law gives sin its power. But thank God! He gives us victory over sin and death through our Lord Jesus Christ.

## THE SAINTLY DEPARTED

Some people have been caught up into heavenly experiences and supernatural encounters in which they've reported speaking with family members in the third heaven, comforted with the peace of God through the experience. Many people on earth right now may be completely oblivious of heaven, and maybe you have been this way in the past, but I can tell you this: the people in heaven, the saints of God there, are not oblivious to what is happening here on the earth. They're very much aware of it all.

The Scriptures speak about martyrs in heaven being able to see current events on earth. These martyrs shouted to the Lord, saying, *"How long, Sovereign Lord, holy and true, until you judge the inhabitants of the earth and avenge our blood?"* (Revelation 6:10). The book of Revelation contains the record of the city of Babylon being destroyed, and an angel pointing to the destruction on earth and instructing the residents of heaven to rejoice. These heavenly saints are able to behold earthly activity and rejoice as God's justice comes to pass. Revelation 18:20 says, *"Rejoice over her, you heavens! Rejoice, you people of God! Rejoice, apostles and prophets! For God has judged her with the judgment she imposed on you."*

> MANY PEOPLE ON EARTH RIGHT NOW MAY BE COMPLETELY OBLIVIOUS OF HEAVEN, AND MAYBE YOU HAVE BEEN THIS WAY IN THE PAST, BUT I CAN TELL YOU THIS: THE PEOPLE IN HEAVEN, THE SAINTS OF GOD THERE, ARE NOT OBLIVIOUS TO WHAT IS HAPPENING HERE ON THE EARTH.

We can visualize these saints in heaven, looking down and beholding the activity on earth. Not only is God allowing us to have encounters in the heavens, but He's also allowing heaven to encounter earth. It is the response to Jesus's prayer: *"Thy kingdom come, Thy will be done in earth, as it is in heaven"* (Matthew 6:10 KJV). Heaven is visiting the earth in this day. We're seeing unusual manifestations, supernatural signs, and miracles of divine healing. And we're seeing divine provision, prosperity for God's people coming to earth from heaven, miracles of divine transfer, and exchange from the supernatural realm into the natural realm.

I find it very interesting what the writer said in Hebrews 12:1–2:

*Therefore, since we are surrounded by such a great cloud of witnesses, let us throw off everything that hinders and the sin that so easily entangles. And let us run with perseverance the race marked out for us, fixing our eyes on Jesus, the pioneer and perfecter of faith. For the joy set before him he endured the cross, scorning its shame, and sat down at the right hand of the throne of God.*

We are surrounded by a great cloud—a cloud of witnesses.

We've been learning about the cloud—the cloud of God's glory, His presence, His blessing, His miracles, His goodness, and His revelation and wisdom—but I want to tell you that it is also a cloud of witnesses. Over the past few years, heaven has been sending me gifts and deposits, impartations and revelations. In response, I have said, "God, I want whatever You have, whatever You want to bring, and how ever You want to bring it. I receive it. I receive from the cloud of Your goodness and blessing."

We are surrounded by the great cloud of witnesses, as the saints watch from their perspective in heavenly glory. These saints, patriarchs, and ancients have been surrounding us and are watching, beholding, and cheering us on. We are surrounded as we run this race. Yes, these revered saints all lived exemplary lives that should help guide our pilgrimage of faith by example, but they also surround us, cheering us on, as our greatest celestial fans!

> WE ARE SURROUNDED BY THE GREAT CLOUD OF WITNESSES, AS THE SAINTS WATCH FROM THEIR PERSPECTIVE IN HEAVENLY GLORY. THESE SAINTS, PATRIARCHS, AND ANCIENTS HAVE BEEN SURROUNDING US AND ARE WATCHING, BEHOLDING, AND CHEERING US ON.

Evangelist Greg Laurie compares it to a marathon, and says, "Many times, after the fastest runners cross the finish line, they stick around to cheer on those who are bringing up the rear. The point is not to see who *won* the race, but to celebrate everyone who *finishes*."[2]

Jacob's life is a great example of finishing the course well in the end, even if there may have been character flaws to work through during the journey. Remember, you are in a spiritual process of discovering who you are in the Spirit. Don't become discouraged or distracted by your character flaws. We all have cracks, but just like the beautiful Japanese kintsukuroi art form, which restores broken pieces of pottery by filling the cracks with golden joinery, making them a much more valued and sought-after treasure, the Spirit is also restoring us as He fills the weaknesses in our life with His glory. The Spirit is moving in us, and working on us, as we allow ourselves to move in glory realms. And we have a celestial grandstand of spiritual heroes cheering us on in the process!

These are our forerunners. This cloud of glory is made up of holy champions who went before us in faith (even though they did not receive the fullness of what had been promised). You can read about them in Hebrews 11, an entire chapter dedicated to their exploits. For instance, Enoch, in verse 5, was a champion of walking by faith, choosing to please God rather than man. Noah, in verse 7, was an example of faith's obedience in the face of ridicule. In verse 8, he was an example of faith's direction. Sarah, in verse 11, was an example of faith's conclusion. Isaac, in verse 20, was an example of faith overcoming fleshly desire. Joseph, in verse 22, was an example of waiting by faith, pursuing, persisting and standing in faith. Moses's parents, in verse 23, were an example of faith overcoming the fear of man. Moses himself, in verses 24–27, was a champion of faith overcoming the praise of man. Israel, in verse 29, was an example of faith's obedience. Rahab, in verse 31, was also an example of faith's conclusion. These great men and women were all champions of faith.

## A GREAT CLOUD OF WITNESSES

*…we also are compassed about with so great a cloud of witnesses…*
(Hebrews 12:1 KJV)

This word *cloud* that is used in Hebrews 12:1 is translated from the Greek word *nephos*. It describes clouds, just like the fluffy, white clouds that you would see in the sky above, but it also has another meaning. In ancient Greece, the word *clouds* was used to describe the highest seats in the bleachers of a stadium. Those seats at the very top of the stadium were called "the clouds," because they were so high up in the air.

The phrase *"compassed about"* is taken from the Greek word *peikeimenai*, which means "to be completely encircled by something that is piled high all around you on every single side." So, this verse carries the following idea: "wherefore seeing we have lying all around us on every side these biblical examples of great faith, they are cheering us on all the way up to the highest heights of heaven." We are running the race, and they are watching us. We know that the Spirit is always watching, and we know that He sends angels to minister to us, to watch over and protect us. But the Scriptures also give us the understanding that these saints of faith, great men and women of God, are also standing over and watching us from a distance.

These saints of old are not concerned with unimportant day-to-day matters—whether or not you checked your email this morning, what clothes you decided to wear, or what you served your dog for dinner. The Scriptures seem to indicate that they focus on decisions that are made in regard to salvation, and also pivotal spiritual moments of increase and achievement—our successes in God. This great cloud of witnesses exists for one reason: to encourage us in pursuing the purposes of God.

The saints of old are able to bring us messages and gifts and even mantels, but this is orchestrated by God, and not something that we should try to pursue on our own merit. First Corinthians 15:47–49 says, *"The first man was of the dust of the earth; the second man is of heaven. As was the earthly man, so are those who are of the earth; and as is the heavenly man, so also are those who are of heaven. And just as we have borne the image of the earthly man, so shall we bear the image of the heavenly man."* We understand from this that those who are in the cloud are not operating with an earthly mind-set or intellect. They are heavenly minded. But even though they are heavenly minded, at times, God allows them to see into the earthly realm in regard to His heavenly purposes being accomplished in our lives.

## MESSAGES FROM THE REALM BEYOND

*But you have come to Mount Zion, to the city of the living God, the heavenly Jerusalem. You have come to thousands upon thousands of angels in joyful assembly, to the church of the firstborn, whose names are written in heaven. You have come to God, the Judge of all, to the spirits of the righteous made perfect, to Jesus the mediator of a new covenant, and to the sprinkled blood that speaks a better word than the blood of Abel.* (Hebrews 12:22–24)

The great cloud of witnesses is not an experience that may or may not happen. It is something that, even now, is surrounding our lives every single day, whether we are aware of it or not. In the glory realm, we are sometimes given the opportunity to have glimpses into that realm of eternity that already surrounds our life. Daniel had a glimpse into that realm. He had a vision in which he saw the ancients speaking to one another. That was his encounter with the cloud.

John had a similar encounter, as recorded in Revelation 22. He was having a series of encounters in the heavens, and he thought he saw an angel, one that was so beautiful that his immediate reaction was to bow down and worship it. Here is the story in his own words:

> I, John, am the one who heard and saw these things. And when I had heard and seen them, I fell down to worship at the feet of the angel who had been showing them to me. (Revelation 22:8)

This messenger had been speaking to John, showing him things, giving him vision and revelation, but in verse 9, he recorded: *"But he said to me, 'Don't do that! I am a fellow servant with you and with your fellow prophets and with all who keep the words of this scroll. Worship God!'"* This was an ancient prophet whom John had encountered in the heavenly realm, who identified himself and advised John to always worship God.

We never worship members of the great cloud of witnesses, we never worship angels, we never worship miracles, and we never worship the things that come from heaven. Instead, we worship the One who is the light of heaven! We worship Jesus Christ—Him and Him alone.

This was a strange encounter that John had, but according to Hebrews 12, we might have a similar encounter. The great cloud of witnesses that surrounds us constantly may well bring us a message from God.

> WE NEVER WORSHIP THE THINGS THAT COME FROM HEAVEN. INSTEAD, WE WORSHIP THE ONE WHO IS THE LIGHT OF HEAVEN! WE WORSHIP JESUS CHRIST—HIM AND HIM ALONE.

## SEEK FIRST HIS KINGDOM

I assure you that I'm not talking about necromancy or summoning the dead here. That is forbidden to God's people:

*When you enter the land the LORD your God is giving you, do not
learn to imitate the detestable ways of the nations there. Let no one be
found among you who sacrifices their son or daughter in the fire, who
practices divination or sorcery, interprets omens, engages in witchcraft, or casts spells, or who is a medium or spiritist or who consults
the dead. Anyone who does these things is detestable to the LORD;
because of these same detestable practices the LORD your God will
drive out those nations before you. You must be blameless before the
LORD your God.* (Deuteronomy 18:9–13)

Necromancy is a sin, and the Scriptures make that clear. It is a
form of dark magic in which the practitioner seeks to summon the
spirit of a deceased person, either as an apparition or a ghost. Often,
the "person" they are attempting to communicate with is actually a
demonic spirit, or familiar spirit, posing as someone who has died. The
Bible says that if you do these things you are *"detestable to the LORD."* So,
we do not engage in witchcraft. We do not engage in speaking with
the dead. We do not engage in conjuring up dead people to speak with
them.

In the glory, we are not permitted to communicate with the dead,
and we do not summon them. And yet, when Jesus was crucified,
we read about some strange events that took place. In Jesus's final
moments on the cross, He gave up His Spirit, and as He did, several
interesting things occurred.

*At that moment the curtain of the temple was torn in two from top
to bottom. The earth shook, the rocks split and the tombs broke open.
The bodies of many holy people who had died were raised to life. They
came out of the tombs after Jesus' resurrection and went into the holy
city and appeared to many people.* (Matthew 27:51–53)

Isn't that interesting! After Jesus's resurrection, these resurrected
saints went into the Holy City and appeared to many people. Who
were these people? They were men and women who had been sleeping
(others said they had died), and the fact that these sleeping saints rose
up and appeared to many created quite a stir. It was very controversial
and scandalous (some things never change).

Mark recorded an exchange between Jesus and some Sadducees. They asked Jesus a hypothetical question about seven brothers who died, one by one. Each time, the wife of the man who had died married the next brother in line, as was the custom of the day. When all of the brothers had died and the woman had died too, the Sadducees asked Jesus, *"At the resurrection whose wife will she be, since the seven were married to her?"* (Mark 12:23). Jesus's response was this:

> *Are you not in error because you do not know the Scriptures or the power of God? When the dead rise, they will neither marry nor be given in marriage; they will be like the angels in heaven. Now about the dead rising—have you not read in the Book of Moses, in the account of the burning bush, how God said to him, "I am the God of Abraham, the God of Isaac, and the God of Jacob"? He is not the God of the dead, but of the living. You are badly mistaken!* (verses 24-27)

*"He is not the God of the dead, but of the living."* We're not calling upon the dead, we're not attempting to summon them, and we're not trying to pull them up and communicate with them. But God has a living cloud of witnesses that surrounds our lives continuously, a cloud of saints who are alive and well in the heavenly realm. Our God is not the God of the dead, but of the living, as Jesus said.

This is not necromancy. We don't seek the dead. We seek the living. It's spiritually immoral for a believer to speak with the dead. We seek Jesus Christ because He is not dead. He is alive! John wrote, *"Jesus answered, 'I am the way and the truth and the life. No one comes to the Father except through me'"* (John 14:6), and *"I am the resurrection and the life. The one who believes in me will live, even though they die"* (John 11:25). Jesus ended this with an important question: *"Do you believe this?"* (verse 26). It's a good question, isn't it? Do you believe these truths that are revealed through the Holy Scriptures? The Bible says that if we believe in Christ, we will not die but have eternal life. So, there are no dead people in heaven, and there are no dead people

> GOD HAS A LIVING CLOUD OF WITNESSES THAT SURROUNDS OUR LIVES CONTINUOUSLY, A CLOUD OF SAINTS WHO ARE ALIVE AND WELL IN THE HEAVENLY REALM. OUR GOD IS NOT THE GOD OF THE DEAD, BUT OF THE LIVING.

in the cloud. That might be hard for you to accept, because religion has taught you differently.

There have been individuals who came to me over the years sharing experiences that they were not able to understand because nobody had shown it to them in the Scriptures. Religion had taught them that what they were experiencing was bad, that it was demonic, that they were operating under dark occult powers. I am not promoting talking to those who have passed away. Don't call on them; call on the name of Jesus. He's the One we can call on.

When I call on Jesus, the Scriptures give me a promise: *"Seek first his kingdom and his righteousness, and all these things will be given to you as well"* (Matthew 6:33). We look to Jesus, the Author and the Finisher, meaning the Author and "Perfecter," of our faith. We call on Him, but we must understand that as we call on Jesus, He will, by His grace, allow us to have encounters with the great cloud of witnesses. These experiences may well go beyond what we have understood in the past.

## GLORIOUS ENCOUNTERS IN THE REALM OF THE LIVING

I'll never forget sitting with Dr. Oral Roberts in his living room in Newport Beach, California, not long before he passed to heavenly glory. I was with a group of ministers who had been invited to ask him questions and allow him to pour his wisdom into our lives. At the end of our time with him, he laid hands on each of us and released an impartation. It was a wonderful experience, one that I will never forget.

As I listened to Dr. Roberts that afternoon, sharing so much divine experience, it seemed that everything that came out of his mouth was a nugget of gold. I took as many notes as I could, as fast as I could write. Then, out of the blue, he said to us, "Oftentimes, I feel my wife, Evelyn, in the house still. She comes and visits me." That was all he said about it, then he went on to other subjects. But that was enough to cause me to realize that he had experienced the cloud. Evelyn was not dead. Although she had passed on to glory, she was alive and well in the heavens. Dr. Oral Robert's face seemed to glow with comfort when he spoke about her still being there in the house near to him.

A few years earlier, I was one of the main speakers at the annual Catch The Fire Conference in Toronto, and at the time, my friend Dr. Harold Beyer was in the hospital in Tampa, Florida. Many of us knew that he had been in the hospital for more than a month and was making the transition into heavenly glory. I was leading praise and worship on the platform at the end of one of the meetings when I closed my eyes and suddenly saw Harold before me. He was walking into the cloud. I knew in that moment that he had joined that great host of witnesses. I could see it.

I walked off the platform and went down to the front row where my armorbearer was seated with my books and my cellphone. I leaned over and said to him, "Harold just passed into glory. I saw it."

He said, "I just got a text from Janet. She said that Harold is with Jesus."

My friend Patricia King has had encounters with the likes of Maria Woodworth-Etter and Kathryn Booth. When I traveled with our friend Chris Harvey, a great evangelist in Australia, he shared with me, night after night, about encounters he'd had with Kathryn Kuhlman. At times, he was aware of her presence, as she would come to impart into his life and release a healing anointing. This seems so unusual to us that we are often not sure if we should even talk about it. Maybe we should just keep it quiet and not tell anyone. I must admit that, until now, I haven't shared this teaching much in public meetings, other than in our International Glory Institute schools, but I know that this is the day of the cloud, and that when the cloud shows up, the fullness of the cloud comes with it, and we must be ready for it.

We don't worship the saints of the past. We don't worship the ones who have gone on before. We worship Jesus. But He has a way of ministering to us in unusual ways, even releasing giftings and mantles through the saints of old.

> WE DON'T WORSHIP THE SAINTS OF THE PAST. WE DON'T WORSHIP THE ONES WHO HAVE GONE ON BEFORE. WE WORSHIP JESUS.

Whenever one of the witnesses in the cloud releases a gifting or a mantle, they release it at the level they had it when they were operating on earth. They don't give it to you the way they got it. They give it to you the way they left it. But you can take it, run further, and do even more. In his book, *Angels on Assignment*, Pastor Roland Buck shared testimonies about encounters he had with Moses and other great biblical figures. Can that be? Of course, because they're all part of the cloud. We shouldn't be surprised by this.

I had the privilege of sitting down with Sister Gwen Shaw in Ashland, Virginia, when she was already eighty-four years old (she passed on to glory at the age of eighty-nine in early 2013). She shared with us that day many of the encounters she'd had. On her eighty-fourth birthday, she recalled, she was lying in bed with her eyes closed when suddenly she could hear a sound in the back of her head. It was like a heavenly orchestra, and then she could hear someone singing. She recognized the voice as that of her beloved Papa Jim, her husband of many years, who had preceded her to glory. He was singing better than she had ever heard him sing before. God had sent him to encourage her on her birthday. What a sweet love-gift from heaven!

## WHAT HAPPENS TO THE DEAD?

Luke recorded the story of the rich man and Lazarus (see Luke 16:19–30), giving us an insight into those who are in hell. It shows us that those who have gone to hell cannot cross back over into the earth (and they certainly cannot cross over into heaven). *"A great chasm has been set in place"* (verse 16) to prevent it. This lets us know that when a person has died and gone to hell, and later seems to be appearing to the living, this is a demonic spirit, or what Scriptures call a *"familiar spirit."* That is not a God encounter. The dead have no access to the earth.

From reading Luke 16, we learn that one of the torments in hell is that those who are there can actually see the earth; they just can't access it. They are aware of those they have left behind who are following in their same sinful footsteps, they know where these loved ones are headed, and they know there's nothing they can do about it. What horrendous torment that must be!

# TEST THE SPIRITS

The Bible warns us to be careful in this regard: *"Test the spirits"* (1 John 4:1). It is not acceptable for anyone to operate with familiar spirits or get involved in demonic activities. What I'm sharing with you is pure, holy, and heavenly. If you test the spirits, you can know if your experience is from God.

While He was living on earth, Jesus had an encounter with the cloud:

> [Jesus said,] *"Truly I tell you, some who are standing here will not taste death before they see the kingdom of God." About eight days after Jesus said this, he took Peter, John and James with him and went up onto a mountain to pray. As he was praying, the appearance of his face changed, and his clothes became as bright as a flash of lightning. Two men, Moses and Elijah, appeared in glorious splendor, talking with Jesus. They spoke about his departure, which he was about to bring to fulfillment at Jerusalem. Peter and his companions were very sleepy, but when they became fully awake, they saw his glory and the two men standing with him. As the men were leaving Jesus, Peter said to him, "Master, it is good for us to be here. Let us put up three shelters—one for you, one for Moses and one for Elijah." (He did not know what he was saying.) While he was speaking, a cloud appeared and covered them, and they were afraid as they entered the cloud. A voice came from the cloud, saying, "This is my Son, whom I have chosen; listen to him." When the voice had spoken, they found that Jesus was alone. The disciples kept this to themselves and did not tell anyone at that time what they had seen.* (Luke 9:27–36)

While Jesus was praying on that mountain, His countenance changed. (The glory of God will change your appearance and your perspective.) Moses and Elijah suddenly appeared before Jesus and began speaking to Him. They had been in Paradise, but through this supernatural encounter, they came back into the natural, earthly realm for a little while. They appeared for a particular purpose: to speak about a significant event in Jesus's earthly life. Then they began to minister to Him about the events that would follow.

Jesus wasn't having a visitation from the *dead*; He was having a visitation from the *living*. One other important thing to note is that Jesus wasn't calling on Moses or Elijah. This was a God encounter that was initiated by heaven for eternal purposes. We do not call on the names of saints of old in order for them to visit us. We do not call on the names of angels in prayer. We do not call on any other name except the name of Jesus. When we do, He will visit us in His glory in new and unusual ways.

> WE DO NOT CALL ON ANY OTHER NAME EXCEPT THE NAME OF JESUS. WHEN WE DO, HE WILL VISIT US IN HIS GLORY IN NEW AND UNUSUAL WAYS.

## GREATER GLORY

One encounter with glory changes everything. In the Spirit, new things are birthed, new callings, giftings, and anointings come to us, and the Spirit prepares us to be a blessing to the nations, to be utilized in a miraculous way. This book is a divine connection for your next dimension. Prepare to be launched into the greatest miracles you've ever known, to be thrust into the greatest days you've ever seen.

Your faith has been increased, God has placed His Spirit upon you and anointed you for this "now moment." Allow the heavy weight of glory to settle upon your life, and, from this day forward, you must walk, run, and soar within the cloud of His goodness. Your eyes are being filled with renewed vision. You have permission to explore every good and perfect sphere of divine presence. You carry a new sound and a new song. The old has passed away, and perpetual promises are opening for you now.

In the days ahead, you will be able to reach into the third heaven and pull a thing down simply by saying, "It's mine." New arenas of provision are available for you. Prosperity is no longer a problem, because you have discovered the inward source of all supply. You will draw from that well, and the miraculous will flow with ease. Where the Spirit of the Lord is, there is freedom. You are a carrier of the glory, a dispenser of wisdom and truth, because the glory lives in you. You will walk upon the waters of the impossible and do the unexplainable. The Spirit will create solid steps under your feet, and you will be led step by step, from faith to faith, anointing to anointing, and from glory to glory, one miracle to the next. *Your journey has only just begun, and all of heaven is cheering you on.*

## FOUND IN CHRIST

When we are found in Christ, we will not experience death. To the contrary, we will experience a rich and satisfying life. Jesus said, in John 10:10 (NLT), *"The thief's purpose is to steal and kill and destroy. My purpose is to give them a rich and satisfying life."*

From the very beginning, mankind was created to live in a perfect place. Originally, that habitation was the garden of Eden. We read about it in Genesis 2:8 (NLT). It says, *"Then the LORD God planted a garden in Eden in the east, and there he placed the man he had made."* We understand from the Scriptures that through the original sin of Adam and Eve, mankind lost the right to live in Paradise. Romans 5:12 (NLT) says it this way: *"When Adam sinned, sin entered the world. Adam's sin brought death, so death spread to everyone, for everyone sinned."* Sin brought with it terrible atrocities, great difficulties, suffering, sickness, poverty, and disconnection from God. Suddenly, man had to work by the sweat of his brow in order to survive. The Bible also says there was a curse placed upon the woman, so that she would have great difficulty and pain in childbearing. Thankfully, the Scriptures revealed to us that Jesus Christ came to break the curse.

## RESTORED TO LIVE AGAIN

When Jesus Christ came to the earth as the last Adam, He reconnected with and restored humanity to an intimate relationship with God. The Bible says we have been reconciled to God. Jesus took upon Himself our sin and our punishment which was separation from God. We didn't deserve what Jesus did for us and did nothing to earn it. Actually, we deserved the opposite. But Jesus traded places with us so we could draw near to God and have fellowship with Him once again, a sweet communion, an intimate relationship.

As Jesus hung on the cross of Calvary, He took upon Himself all of the curse for our wrongdoing: *"But Christ has rescued us from the curse pronounced by the law. When he was hung on the cross, he took upon himself the curse for our wrongdoing. For it is written in the Scriptures, 'Cursed is everyone who is hung on a tree'"* (Galatians 3:13 NLT). Part of this restoration through Jesus Christ is the ability of man to once again live in Paradise with God in a perfect atmosphere, and in perfect harmony, unity, and blessing.

> MANY PEOPLE STRIVE AND STRUGGLE AND DON'T UNDERSTAND THAT GOD DID NOT INTEND FOR THEM TO LIVE IN A CONSTANT CYCLE OF STRUGGLES. HIS INTENTION WAS THAT WE LABOR TO ENTER INTO THE PLACE OF HIS REST.

The Spirit hasn't destined you to live in constant struggle. He hasn't called you to a life of striving. The Scriptures emphatically state, *"Let us, therefore, make every effort to enter that rest, so that no one will perish by following their example of disobedience"* (Hebrews 4:11). Many people strive and struggle and don't understand that God did not intend for them to live in a constant cycle of struggles. His intention was that we labor to enter into the place of His rest. This is bigger than us, greater than our own ability, wider than our own provision, and expands beyond our own vision. God's dreams for us are greater than the dreams we have for ourselves. It's time to connect with God and dream with Him.

The Scriptures challenge us: *"Have the same mindset as Christ Jesus"* (Philippians 2:5). His mind-set is one of truth, revelation, wisdom, understanding, and creativity. In 1 Corinthians 15:45, the Scriptures say, *"The first man Adam became a living being; the last Adam, a life-giving spirit."* We will live eternally with Christ, the last Adam, for He is the life-giving Spirit. There is no death in Him, no destruction in Him, no sin in Him, no darkness in Him. When His Spirit-life comes upon my spirit, when I allow Him access into my heart to become Lord over my life, the life-giving essence of the heavens lives inside of me.

Since Christ is the life-giving Spirit, I will live eternally with Him. If you've never prayed to accept Jesus Christ into your life as your personal Lord and Savior, why don't you pray this prayer now:

Jesus,

Come into my heart. I invite You to be my Lord and Savior. I give You my sin in exchange for the life that only You can give. Thank You for cleansing me with Your blood and giving me a brand new start. I receive this gift of salvation.

Amen!

## DEATH HAS BEEN DEFEATED

I will not die. I will not taste death. I will pass from this realm to the next with ease. Like Enoch, I will walk with the Spirit and just keep on walking. I'll keep going up, up, up! Ephesians 2:6 says, *"For he raised us from the dead along with Christ and seated us with him in the heavenly realms because we are united with Christ Jesus"* (NLT). Therefore, Paul could say, *"I have been crucified with Christ and I no longer live, but Christ lives in me. The life I now live in the body, I live by faith in the Son of God, who loved me and gave himself for me"* (Galatians 2:20). He raises us up by His act of victory over death.

When Jesus rose from the dead, I was there with Him, being raised up into a new place of life, into a new place of resurrection glory, into a new place of living. This is not something that's *about to happen*. It's something's that's *already happened*. I was there with Him, and He was there with me.

When Jesus rose, I rose too. When He conquered death, I conquered death as well. Spiritually speaking, I have risen with Him to sit with Him in heavenly places. I may be sitting here on earth writing this book, but my spirit sits in another dimension. You might see me here now, but I'm living in another place. You might call me a Canadian citizen, but I'm a stranger in this world, a foreigner on this earth. I don't belong to this planet. I come from another sphere altogether. I am a citizen of heaven because I've been seated with Christ in heavenly places.

No wonder we desire to soar!

No wonder we vibrate at a higher frequency!

No wonder we want to always be in the glory with our Savior!

No wonder we set our affections on Him!

Jesus said it like this: *"It is finished!"* (John 19:30). Yes, it is finished! It's not *about to be* finished. It's not a work in progress. You're not fighting *for* the victory; you're living *from* the victory. The greatest spiritual warfare you can do this day is stand in the glory, covered by God's anointing, believing the Word of Truth that you are everything He dreamed you would be, that every promise in the Scriptures belongs to you, and that everything He has said about you is coming to pass.

Moses said it well: *"God is not human, that he should lie, not a human being, that he should change his mind. Does he speak and then not act? Does he promise and not fulfill?"* (Numbers 23:19). God said, *"I am watching to see that my word is fulfilled"* (Jeremiah 1:12). He is looking for people who will simply believe Him.

That's why I love the atmosphere of glory. As you step into it, the reality of God comes alive. You see things you have never seen, even though they were there the whole time. We are situated in eternal realms where the possibilities of eternity become our present reality. God made heaven for us, and He made us for heaven. We belong in this heavenly realm. Reach all the way into the glory, and allow this glory to reach all the way into you.

I want you to put into practice the things I've shared in this book. Allow the wheel to turn within you. As the Spirit moves, it requires some moving on your part as well. Let the Spirit make the necessary changes in your life, so you can embrace these dimensions of His goodness fully.

Now, in closing, please pray with me:

Father God,

Thank You for introducing us to these glory realms. We receive every inspired word and revelation from heaven. Let praise and worship arise with a new song from our lips. Surround our lives with Your angelic helpers from above. Let Your power and miracles flow through our touch, even as we embrace Your cloud of glory, which brings the greater rains of the miraculous.

Guide us in fully embracing Your blessing, favor, and increase, so that we might be generous on every occasion. We surrender to Your leading as You lift us up to soar in realms of the Spirit. Fill our vision with a revelation of heavenly glory. Let Your goodness come forth in our lives as we yield to the work of Your greater glory.

In the precious name of Jesus.

Amen!

Are you hungry to go deeper in the Spirit? He has greater things prepared for you as you determine to enter into these *Glory Realms*.

# ENDNOTES

## INTRODUCTION
1. Analyzed by Andrew Hajash, Jr., Department of Geology and Geophysics, Texas A&M University, August 23, 1999.

## CHAPTER 1
1. See https://www.merriam-webster.com/dictionary/faith (accessed 10/23/2017).
2. See https://www.merriam-webster.com/dictionary/substance (accessed 10/23/2017).
3. See http://www.pbs.org/faithandreason/theogloss/logos-body.html (accessed 10/23/2017).
4. F. F. Bosworth, *Christ the Healer* (Grand Rapids, MI: Fleming H. Revell, 1973) 49.
5. Lyrics from "Changing the Atmosphere," words and music by Steve Swanson, (4th Door Productions, 2009).
6. The Eastern Arctic Bible Conference, April 2004.

## CHAPTER 2
1. *Strong's* "mashach," Hebrew #4886.
2. *Receive Your Healing* by Joshua Mills and Steve Swanson, 2017. Distributed by Spiritual Technologies & Advanced Training Systems. Available for purchase online at: www.joshuamills.com.

## CHAPTER 3
1. Guillermo Maldonado, *The Glory of God* (New Kensington, Pennsylvania:Whitaker House, 2012), 70.

2. Earlier in history the Hawaiian Islands were a kingdom ruled by a monarchy and, therefore, they are spiritually recognized as a nation. https://en.wikipedia.org/wiki/Kingdom_of_Hawaii (accessed 12/20/2017).

## CHAPTER 4

1. A group of fifteen psalms, comprised of chapters 120–134.
2. https://en.wikipedia.org/wiki/Song_of_Ascents (accessed May 3, 2018).
3. Ruth Ward Heflin, *Glory: Experiencing the Atmosphere of Heaven* (Hagerstown, MD: McDougal Publishing, 1990), front matter.
4. Pat Kenny (Illustrator), this image was released by the National Cancer Institute, an agency part of the National Institutes of Health, with the ID 2512, https://en.wikipedia.org/wiki/Cancer_cell (accessed May 9, 2018).
5. Margaret Ann Rorke, Ph.D., "Music and the Wounded of World War II," *Journal of Music Therapy*, vol. 33, issue 3 (October 1, 1996) 189–207.
6. See https://www.health.harvard.edu/blog/healing-through-music-20151105 (accessed May 9, 2018).
7. See https://futurism.com/is-music-in-our-dna (accessed May 9, 2018).
8. Joshua Mills, *Simple Supernatural* (Maricopa, AZ: XP Publishing, 2010). Available at www.joshuamills.com.

## CHAPTER 5

1. Brenda Redmond, *My Journey as I Walk Unknown Paths* (Lulu Publishing Company, 2012).
2. Available for download from www.joshuamills.com.
3. Roy Hicks, *Guardian Angels* (Tulsa, OK: Harrison House, Inc., 1991).

## CHAPTER 6

1. The word *saved* comes from the Greek word *sozo*, which means save, heal, preserve and rescue. It is clear from this definition that salvation includes the healing of physical ailments.
2. Charles and Frances Hunter, *How to Heal the Sick* (New Kensington, PA: Whitaker House, 2012) 126.
3. *Holman Bible Dictionary* (Nashville, TN: Broadman & Holman, 1991).

## CHAPTER 7

1. The words *blessing, blessed,* and *bless* are used 640 times in the King James Version.
2. Malachi 3:8–12 needs to be understood in the light of Galatians 3:13–14. God gives us grace to tithe, but we are never to do it under ungodly pressure or manipulation. The curse has been destroyed, and now, under the new covenant, we tithe because the blessing has already been secured. We have no fear of lack or curse. And, because we are blessed, we can be a blessing.

3. See http://www.businessinsider.com/most-generous-people-in-the-world-2015-10 (accessed May 10, 2018).
4. Heflin, 19–20.
5. According to the *Dake Annotated Reference Bible*.

## CHAPTER 8

1. See https://factualfacts.com/chicken-longest-recorded-flight (accessed May 10, 2018)..
2. BBC News, October 2, 2014, "Wonga to write off £220m of customer debts," http://www.bbc.co.uk/news/business-29457044 (accessed May 10, 2018).
3. "Diamond Days," *Time*, Canadian edition, April 5, 2004.

## CHAPTER 9

1. See https://spaceplace.nasa.gov/troposphere/en (accessed 12/06/2017).
2. Greg Laurie, *As It Is in Heaven* (Colorado Springs, CO: NavPress, 2014), 115.

# ABOUT THE AUTHOR

Joshua Mills is an internationally recognized ordained minister of the gospel, as well as a recording artist, keynote conference speaker, and author of more than twenty books and spiritual training manuals. He is well known for his unique insights into the glory realm, prophetic sound, and the supernatural atmosphere that he carries. Wherever Joshua ministers, the Word of God is confirmed by miraculous signs and wonders that testify of Jesus Christ. For more than twenty years, he has helped people discover the life-shifting truth of salvation, healing, and deliverance for spirit, soul and body. Joshua and his wife, Janet, cofounded International Glory Ministries, and have ministered on six continents in over seventy-five nations around the world. Featured in several film documentaries and print articles, including *Charisma* and *Worship Leader Magazine*, together, they have ministered to millions around the world through radio, television, and online webcasts, including appearances on TBN, Daystar, GodTV, *It's Supernatural! with Sid Roth, 100 Huntley Street*, and *Everlasting Love with Patricia King*. Their ministry is located in both Palm Springs, California, and London, Ontario, Canada, where they live with their three children: Lincoln, Liberty, and Legacy.

To contact the author for ministry invitations, resources, upcoming spiritual training seminars or prayer please contact:

International Glory Ministries
P.O. Box 4037
Palm Springs, CA 92263
www.JoshuaMills.com